TEACHING SECONDARY ENGLISH WITH ICT

5·2008

Learning and Teaching with Information and Communications Technology

Series Editors: Anthony Adams and Sue Brindley

The role of ICT, in the curriculum, is much more than simply a passing trend. It provides a real opportunity for teachers of all phases and subjects to rethink fundamental pedagogical issues alongside the approaches to learning that pupils need to apply in classrooms. In this way it foregrounds the ways in which teachers can match in school the opportunities for learning provided in the home and community. The series is firmly rooted in practice and also explores the theoretical underpinning of the ways in which curriculum content and skills can be developed by the effective integration of ICT in schooling. It addresses the educational needs of the early years, the primary phase and secondary subject areas. The books are appropriate for preservice teacher training and continuing professional development, as well as for those pursuing higher degrees in education.

Published and forthcoming titles:

A. Adams and S. Brindley (eds): *Teaching Secondary English with ICT*
R. Barton (ed.): *Teaching Secondary Science with ICT*
L. Florian and J. Hegarty (eds): *ICT and Special Educational Needs*
M. Hayes and D. Whitebread (eds): *ICT in the Early Years*
S. Johnston-Wilder and D. Pimm (eds): *Teaching Secondary Mathematics with ICT*
A. Loveless and B. Dore (eds): *ICT in the Primary School*
M. Monteith (ed.): *Teaching Primary Literacy with ICT*
M. Monteith (ed.): *Teaching Secondary School Literacies with ICT*
P. Warwick, E. Wilson and M. Winterbottom (eds): *Teaching and Learning Primary Science with ICT*
J. Way and T. Beardon (eds): *ICT and Primary Mathematics*

TEACHING SECONDARY ENGLISH WITH ICT

Edited by

Anthony Adams and Sue Brindley

 Open University Press

Open University Press
McGraw-Hill Education
Shoppenhangers Road
Maidenhead
Berkshire
England
SL6 2QL

email: enquiries@openup.co.uk
world wide web: www.openup.co.uk

and Two Penn Plaza, New York, NY 10121-2289, USA

First Published 2007

A catalogue record of this book is available from the British Library

ISBN-10: 0 335 21444 4 (pb)   0 335 21445 2 (hb)
ISBN-13: 978 0 335 21444 0 (pb)   978 0 335 21445 7 (hb)

Library of Congress Cataloging-in-Publication Data
CIP data applied for

Typeset by RefineCatch Limited, Bungay, Suffolk
Printed in Poland by OZ Graf. S.A.
www.polskabook.pl

*Every effort has been made to trace and acknowledge the copyright holders of material
reproduced in this book but if any infringement has occurred then this will be rectified at
the first opportunity if notice is given to the publishers.*

The **McGraw·Hill** Companies

CONTENTS

SERIES EDITORS' PREFACE

Of all subjects, English must be the one which poses simultaneously most problems and most opportunities for using ICT in the classroom: most problems because it is a subject which is oracy based, and so many times, though hopefully not in the English classroom, the use of computers is interpreted in the classroom as an individual, screen focused and, sadly, silent (except for the tapping of keys) event; most opportunity because English is a subject ready to think about new ways of constructing reading and writing; about the pedagogical value of collaborative work and the possibilities afforded by the renaissance of learning made possible through ICT.

English, and English teachers (and we mean by this all those teaching English, media and drama), have of course thrived on being different. In a subject which deals with values and beliefs it would be a depressing state of affairs if we were relegated to the transmission of correct ways of punctuating text, or caring overly about the right uses of prefixes and suffixes. These are important: we would want to acknowledge that. But they are not at the heart of English. The dilemma perhaps is that ICT loans itself very well to the surface correction of text. Spell and grammar checks (with the caveats of the nonsenses that can be caused by the application of rules above sense that computers can come up with) enable a; focus on these areas which was not available before ICT. But ICT can do so much more. It is not, as Davies cautions, a 'solution' to bring about effective English

teaching: only when teachers understand the deep pedagogy of their subject (and these will be teachers who will be acknowledged as expert practitioners) can we see ICT being used with real impact: good use of and
knowledge about ICT is actually very little to do with understanding the
technology: it helps, of course, to know about new software packages
which allow you to annotate text but it will still take a good teacher to
know when and where this feature will allow students to learn in more
effective ways. But perhaps most exciting is when English teachers are
freed by ICT to consider how speaking and listening can be an integral part
of work with computers, as Mercer et al explore; how writing can move
beyond the individually produced text, or reading be re-visioned (and we
do mean this term) to include graphics, hypertext and texts which only
'end' when the reader decides so to do; when teaching texts in the classroom can allow students to engage with ideas such as literary theory
which once were the preserve of university undergraduate teaching– and
to do so in ways which promote afar deeper understanding of text than the
standard literary analysis can.

So we expect the use of ICT in the English classroom to be controversial:
it would be disappointing if English teachers did not actively debate their
subject and the dynamics of change. Our hope is that this volume contributes to those debates, offers an account of where research has illumin-
ated ICT and English teaching, explores ideas about reading and writing
and ICT within and beyond the UK and challenges thinking about the
ways ICT and English belong together. We hope you enjoy reading the
chapters here (which include contributions from English teachers as well
as those researching the area): but mostly, we hope the debates within and
about English continue, so that new life continues to be breathed into this
most important of subjects, and that the discussions about English and
ICT is one such oxygenating force.

Anthony Adams & Sue Brindley

1

COMPUTERS, LITERACY AND THINKING TOGETHER

N. Mercer, L. Dawes, R. Wegerif, C. Sams and M. Fernandez

Introduction

In this chapter we begin by presenting a particular, socio-cultural perspective on the use of computers in relation to the English curriculum. Next, we explain how this perspective was used in the classroom-based research that provides the basis for this chapter. That research has led us to the conclusion that there are two important aspects of the use of ICT for developing children's awareness and capability in using language. The first is to design activities, using appropriate software, which will enable children to use language to 'think together'. The second is for the teacher to give explicit guidance to children in how to use language to communicate effectively, in ways that take account of the communicative needs of particular audiences, situations and tasks. We illustrate both these aspects with classroom examples from our research projects, and conclude the chapter by summarizing the significance of our analysis for educational practice.

A socio-cultural perspective on education is one which gives particular attention to the roles of language and other 'cultural tools' (Vygotsky 1987) for enabling the development of each new generation. Language is not merely a tool for providing information or facilitating social interaction, it is a tool for collective sense making. It does not merely enable us to interact, it enables us to link minds – to 'interthink' (Mercer 2000). In our view, this conception of language as a tool for thinking together has considerable educational potential, especially when coupled with the affordances of computer technology. The forms of language found in email, computer conferencing and 'texting' with mobile phones, reflect both the nature of the technologies and the communicative purposes to which people apply them. While technological and communicative developments have led to a reconsideration of what is meant by literacy (Rassool 1999; Pailliotet and Mosenthal 2000), it is worth noting that the creation of any digital text still requires a functional competence in written language. If ICT is used as a basis for interesting, meaningful and communicative activities, it can effectively stimulate children's skills in using both spoken and written language.

The socio-cultural perspective has also encouraged a conception of literacy as *social practice* (Heath 1983; Street 1983, 1993; Barton 1994). That is, rather than considering literacy simply in terms of individual cognitive skills, it has been found useful to consider it in terms of functional ways of communicating which are established in a society. In any society, using written language involves more than learning how to decode and encode text. Becoming literate means developing skills for interpreting and creating the texts that are involved in the cultural activities of everyday life. It also involves moving between speech and writing, for example, in interacting with others to make sense of texts.

As technology offers new ways of communicating, it is clear that schools must incorporate these ways into their social, communicative practices. On the other hand, fears are commonly expressed that the aim of enabling students to master the basics of oracy and literacy will be sacrificed to the use of the new technology. As we explain in this chapter, this is not the choice which needs to be made. Computer-based activities can be undertaken in ways which will increase opportunities for children to talk and work together, and develop their skills in both spoken and written language. Moreover, increased educational use of new technologies should not be seen as lessening the importance of dialogue between teachers and learners, though it may increase the range of possible contexts for those dialogues.

The ground rules of educational activity

Let us first focus on spoken language and how this is used in classroom activities. Back in the 1980s, Edwards and Mercer (1987) showed how the familiar patterns of classroom interaction depended on teachers and pupils following a set of implicit norms or 'educational ground rules'. A taken-for-granted understanding of how to behave in class enables events to proceed smoothly. But through a careful analysis of classroom talk, Edwards and Mercer showed that classroom interaction is often not based on a firm foundation of 'common knowledge' and that misunderstandings between teachers and students are common. This can mean that students miss the point of an activity, or that a teacher is not aware that the students lack some understanding which is necessary for the activity to be educationally productive. More specifically, when setting up group-based activity, teachers hardly ever begin by sharing with a class their expectations for how students should interpret an instruction, such as 'talk together', 'discuss this text' or 'work together to solve this problem', perhaps assuming that these matters are self-evident (Mercer 1995). One effect of this is that students often lack a clear understanding of what they are expected to do and why they are doing it. They may have no understanding of what constitutes 'discussion' in educational settings, or how to 'work together'. In the 1990s, classroom-based observational research by ourselves and colleagues, revealed that much of the interaction taking place was not of any obvious educational value (Fisher 1993; Mercer 1994; Wegerif and Scrimshaw 1997). In most cases, the children observed were not discussing their ideas about work and showed little sign of learning from each other. It was common for one child to make all the decisions about how to proceed while the others watched; or children adopted a competitive style and did not collaborate at all.

Drawing on the same concept of 'educational ground rules' in their study of writing in British secondary schools, Sheeran and Barnes (1991) showed how many of the expectations that teachers had about what constitutes a satisfactory essay, scientific report or other kind of written work, were never made explicit to pupils. And even when some of those requirements were made clear, teachers rarely discussed with pupils *why* they were expected to write (or talk) in particular ways. Sheeran and Barnes (1991: 2) therefore concluded: 'In spite of their importance, these tacit expectations or ground rules, are seldom discussed with pupils because the teachers themselves are largely unaware of them.' Bringing the 'ground rules' out into the open could have educational benefits, as Sheeran and Barnes suggested. This has been a basic principle of our own work with teachers in primary and secondary schools.

Exploratory talk

An initial stage of our work with teachers has been to ask them how they would like students to talk when working together in groups. With any group of teachers there is usually a consensus, with teachers agreeing that students should ask each other questions so that opinions are shared, that all members of a group should participate, and that ideas which are shared should be treated respectfully, but be subject to constructive criticism.

In other words, students should be encouraged in such discussions to make all relevant knowledge *publicly accountable*. The kind of interaction which teachers say they would hope to happen, can be called *exploratory talk*. Building on the way this term was first used by Barnes and Todd (1977, 1995), we have defined it as follows:

> Exploratory talk is that in which partners engage critically but constructively with each other's ideas. Relevant information is offered for joint consideration. Proposals may be challenged and counter-challenged, but if so reasons are given and alternatives are offered. Agreement is sought as a basis for joint progress. Knowledge is made publicly accountable and reasoning is visible in the talk.
>
> (Mercer 2000: 98)

We are not suggesting that exploratory talk represents the only mode of interaction which is appropriate in joint activity, but we are convinced that it deserves more attention in school, for two related reasons. The first is that it represents the kind of reasoned discussion that every child should be enabled to engage in. The second is that, despite it matching teachers' own specifications of a 'good discussion', it is a rare phenomenon in most classrooms.

The next stage in our work with teachers is to move on from using the concept of 'educational ground rules' merely to describe the implicit, normative basis of classroom communications to using it prescriptively, to generate a new and explicit basis for productive interaction. We encourage teachers to raise the notion of 'ground rules for talk' with their classes. Teachers are often surprised initially by the idea that children might not understand what is expected of them, but most agree that they seldom, if ever, make the 'ground rules' for discussion explicit in their classes. This leads into a consideration of the role of the teacher in modelling and scaffolding children's use of language and of what constitutes a 'good discussion' among children. From this basis, the concept of exploratory talk can be introduced to the students. The following implementation phase, involves teachers carrying out initial activities with their classes in which they provide direct teaching of speaking and listening skills. The teacher then leads their class to define and agree their own ground rules for talk (related to the concept of exploratory talk), which they go on to use in their collaborative work. An example of such ground rules is provided as Figure 1.1. The children then pursue the rest of a specially designed programme of 'Thinking Together' lessons over a period of approximately ten weeks. These lessons have a consistent format in which teacher-led sessions and group-based activities are integrated, and in which the content of activities is directly related to various subjects of the prescribed school curriculum. (The lessons for primary schools (Key Stage 2) are included in Dawes *et al.* 2000; those for secondary (Key Stage 3) are not yet published).

- Listen to other people because it helps you understand the way they think.
- Take part! Your ideas are as valuable as everyone else's. It is not OK to not take part. Share!
- Treat people fairly – don't interrupt them, don't put them down.
- Criticize the idea, not the person.
- It is all right to change your mind.
- Work together to reach a solution.

Figure 1.1 Ground rules for talk from a secondary class (Year 8)

Computers and literacy practices in school

We have generated several computer-based, literacy-related joint activities to be used with the Thinking Together lessons. Computer-based activities have been found to be motivating and to provide a strong focus for group activity (Hoyles *et al.* 1990; Scrimshaw 1993; Howe *et al.* 1996; Light and Littleton 1999; Littleton and Light 1999). However, the design of particular types of software can strongly influence the quality of group discussion – and research suggests that much software used in schools is not well designed to support joint activity and stimulate collective thinking (Wegerif 1996, 1997). Coupled with students' lack of awareness and understanding about how to conduct a productive discussion, there is a danger that computer-based joint activities will have little practical value for developing their oral and written language. We have responded to this problem in three main ways. First, we have been very careful in selecting software as the basis for thinking together activities. Second, we have designed some new items of software with features specifically calculated to encourage discussion. And third, as we explain below, we have embedded group computer-based activities in teacher-led lessons which are intended to provide a clear, shared understanding among participants of how to talk and work together effectively.

Productive discussion of a narrative text

Some of the Thinking Together lessons are related to literacy development and include group-based activities concerned with the children's understanding of narratives. The aim is to help children move beyond a simple grasp of 'the story' into a deeper consideration of the motives and consequences of the actions of characters and of other possible, hypothetical routes that a narrative could take. One of these, also related to citizenship studies, is a computer-based activity called *Kate's Choice*. The program introduces children to a girl called Kate, whose best friend Robert tells her a secret; he has stolen a box of chocolates from a shop near their school. He says that they are for his mother who is in hospital. Robert begs Kate not to tell. She agrees, but subsequent events make it difficult for her to decide whether this promise should be kept. One frame from *Kate's Choice* is shown as Figure 1.2.

The software design ensures that the children follow the narrative sequence, but at each main stage of its development they are able to interact with it in two ways. First, they can ask characters involved in the story for their views about what Kate should do and what should happen to Robert. They are then asked to discuss whether they agree with these views. Second, they can write into the story their own views on what Kate should do and how Robert's actions should be treated. The phrase 'Talk together and decide . . .' on the computer screen (as shown in Figure 1.2) prompts the children to talk about the alternative choices presented. So at each of several stages in the narrative, the children are asked to jointly consider relevant information at their disposal and the points of view of each of the characters involved, before coming to a decision and proposing what should happen next. The task therefore involves the use of various kinds of language skills. Literacy skills are required in reading the narrative, appreciating the perspectives of the characters involved, and

Figure 1.2 A decision point in *Kate's Choice*

projecting the narrative forward along hypothetical routes which would arise from each possible choice Kate could make; and oral skills are required in making proposals, presenting reasons, listening to the views of others and resolving different points of view.

Having designed *Kate's Choice*, we then evaluated its use as an element of the Thinking Together curriculum activities. We wished to know whether the software was effective in generating a lively and focused discussion, but we also wanted to see whether the quality of discussion was affected by whether children's use of exploratory talk had been 'scaffolded' by their teacher's implementation of the Thinking Together approach. To do this, we observed and video-recorded two sets of children in primary classes in Milton Keynes, a town in south-east England. One set of children were those in 'target classes', who had already taken part in Thinking Together lessons. Their talk was compared with that of children in 'control classes' in similar local schools (matched for aspects of social catchment) who were given the software without any special preparation for discussion. The children all worked in mixed sex and mixed ability groups of three.

Our observations in control schools revealed talk of varying quality, but only very rarely did *Kate's Choice* generate an extended and lively discussion. An extract from a typical discussion in a control school is included as transcript 1 below. The children (all aged 11) have reached the point in the narrative shown in Figure 1.2.

Transcript I : Do that

Jared:	(*reads from screen*) 'Talk together and decide what Kate should do then click on one of the buttons.'
Tony:	What should we do? (*looking towards the teacher*)
Jared:	Do that. (*Jared points at the screen*)
Tony:	(*turning to call the teacher*) Excuse me. (*turning back to group*) We don't know what to do.
Effie:	(*clicks mouse*)
Jared:	Yes we do.

(*Total time: 42 seconds*)

Comment

No members of this group react positively to the computer prompt, 'talk together' (Tony even turns to the teacher for guidance). Effie, who happens to have the mouse, decides the choice for the group. Her assumption of control goes unchallenged and the group move rapidly through the task, rather than really considering the structure of the narrative or the moral issues involved. The opportunity to discover and consider each other's ideas is not pursued.

For comparison, transcript 2 below is an extract from the discussion of a target class group who have had several weeks' involvement in Thinking Together activities. They have arrived at the same decision point in the narrative.

Transcript 2: What do you think?

Gary: Right we've got to talk about it. (*Trish looks at Sue*)
Trish: What do you think? (*Trish points at Gary*)
Sue: What do you think?
Gary: I think even though he is her friend then um she shouldn't tell of him because em well she should tell of him em because was, was, if he's stealing it it's not worth having a friend that steals is it?
Trish: No
Sue: Why do you think that?
Trish: We said why. I think that one as well do you? (*Trish points to the screen and looks at Sue*)
Gary: I think she should tell her parents. Do you? (*Gary looks at Sue*)
Trish: I think I'm I think even though he is her friend because he's stealing she should still tell her parents and her parents might give her the money and she might be able to go to the shop and give them the money
Sue: I think um . . .
Gary: . . . but then she's paying for the thing she stole so I think he should get the money anyway. He should have his . . .
Sue: I think that he should go and tell his mother
Gary: . . . own mother Mum
Trish: Even though she has promised?
Sue: Because he's well you shouldn't break a promise really should you?
Gary: What's it worth having a friend if he's going to steal?
Trish: If he steals. If you know he's stolen if she don't tell her parents then he will be getting away with it (*Trish looking at Sue*)
Gary: It's not worth having a friend that steals is it?
(*3 second pause*)
Sue: OK then (*puts hand on mouse*)
Trish: Ain't worth it is it?
Sue: Tells her parents
Sue: (*clicks mouse*)
Gary: Yeh go on
(*Total time: 109 seconds*)

Comment

Here the instruction 'Talk together and decide . . .' elicits a very different kind of response. This is not perfect exploratory talk; few extra reasons are given in support of the initial position taken by Gary, and it is hard to tell if Sue is persuaded by the reasoning or merely acquiesces to the strength of the majority view. But this discussion has some key features of exploratory talk. The children ask each other for their views and give reasons to support them. They question each other's positions and consider alternatives carefully before taking a shared decision. In these ways, they are implementing their agreed 'ground rules'.

The discussions of the talk in the two groups of transcript 1 and transcript 2 can be contrasted in terms of how this kind of activity might feed into subsequent writing assignments for the children involved. Asked to write an ending to the narrative, the members of the target group (transcript 2) would each have the 'common knowledge' newly created by their discussion as a literary resource. However, members of the control group (transcript 1) would have gained little such resource from their interaction.

We have provided just two contrasting examples, but a qualitative and quantitative analysis of the discourse data, from both target and control schools (as described in more detail in Mercer *et al.* 1999), showed that overall the talk of the target-class groups was significantly more 'exploratory' in nature than the talk of control groups. More precisely, in comparison with control groups, children in target classes did more of the following:

- They asked each other task-focused questions.
- They gave reasons for statements and challenges.
- They spent more time (than control groups) discussing the implications of characters' views and actions for the narrative development.
- They considered more than one possible position before making a decision.
- They elicited opinions from all in the group.
- They reached agreement before acting.

In contrast, the talk of control groups showed more of the following features:

- The child controlling the mouse made unilateral decisions.
- The choice of the most dominant child was accepted without discussion.
- Arbitrary decisions were made without debating the alternatives.
- Children spent very little time at each decision point before moving on.

We concluded that the Thinking Together lessons had encouraged more effective use of language as a tool for reasoning and had enabled children to develop effective ways of exploring a narrative text together. The *Kate's Choice* software had provided a good environment for exercising and developing these oral and literate language skills. Target groups responded to the talk prompts provided by the software as an opportunity to engage with one another's ideas in an 'exploratory' manner. The software was used by the children as a tool for thinking together, and not as a game in which speed of response is important. It supported pupils' engagement with each other's ideas and opinions.

Writing online

In the most recent phase of our research, groups of children in two schools have been communicating with each other electronically. Classes from separate project schools (of children aged 10 and 11) were organized as paired groups, and the Oracle conferencing software *Think.com* was used to set up an online forum for discussion between groups. In this recent research, we have given particular consideration to the way that language is used by the children as they generate email, concept maps and web pages (Fernandez 2001). *Think.com* provides an online environment for sharing ideas and contributing text, data or documents for discussion. The participating schools were provided with email and conferencing links, which comply with standards for Internet safety set by the UK government's Department for Education and Skills (DfES 2000).

The groups' face-to-face and online discussions, were focused on a specific collaborative writing task: the creation of a website about curriculum-related topics. The following extract is an example of an initial message sent by one group to their partners.

> HELLO! . . . We are class 5M which has fifteen children in it, eight boys and seven girls. We are excited about sending you a message and we love reading your replies.
>
> We are hoping that we will be able to help each other with our Science subject after the Easter holidays . . .
>
> Today in our talking lesson we have a group of three people being videoed. We don't know how they are getting on at the moment but we hope they have remembered all the talking lesson rules. . .

The next extract is a response from the partner group which poses questions to sustain the conversation and direct it towards their joint science activities.

> Hello there, we have received your message. Thank you for your short notice. . . In our science lessons we are talking about materials. What are you talking about in science? We have mainly been talking about solids/ liquids/ gases.

The subsequent planning and creation of web pages involved the use of two further commercially produced software packages, which were integrated with the use of *Think.com*. The lesson plans for this work provided teachers with a structure to encourage the children to apply and develop joint reasoning through 'exploratory writing', as they undertook this task.

The children used *eMindMaps* software to plan ideas and draw simple concept maps. These were shared with the partner group and comments were exchanged using *Think.com*. The following extracts from the teachers' notes (as supplied to each teacher by the project team) for the relevant Thinking Together lesson, illustrate what is required of the teacher (see Figure 1.3). The teacher is asked to model exploratory talk in the introductory session and to clarify aims at the start of the group activity. As with all the Thinking Together activities, a closing teacher-led plenary is used to share experience among members of the class and clarify what should happen next.

In other lessons, before and after this one, teachers were also expected to remind children of their agreed 'ground rules' (as described earlier in this chapter), and to encourage their use both within the class and in email exchanges with the partner class, as they researched the content for their web pages. An additional piece of software, *SiteCentral*, was provided to enable children to construct simple web pages by using 'drag and drop' techniques.

Introductory plenary (whole class)
. . . Discuss with the class how to make comments about a concept map and suggest possible changes. Draw a concept map . . . Ask the children to make comments about the map and how it could be improved.

Show them how to construct these comments in a positive way, e.g. "We liked your idea about . . . Do you think that a link showing . . . might be a useful way to . . . ? Can you explain the connection between?
Write some of these comments together.

Group work
. . . Remind them of the ground rules for talk.

Ask the groups to look at their partner group's concept map. Then they should talk together to agree on some comments. Can they think of a question to ask about it? Can they make a suggestion about how it might be changed?

Plenary
The purpose of this plenary session is to create a class concept map that incorporates contributions from all of the groups . . . Ask each group in turn to suggest one of their ideas and to explain its relationships. Each group could also explain one part of their partner group's map. As the contributions are made, record these onto the map. In this way the children will be able to see the relationships between all of the contributions. When the map is finished it should collate all the ideas from the groups . . .

Figure 1.3 Extracts from teachers' notes for concept map lesson

The teachers and children who worked on this phase of the project encountered some practical problems, mainly related to the constraints of time and the ability to maintain ongoing contact with the partner class. These are common problems in computer-based educational activity. Despite these difficulties, the teachers reported that they found the approach an exciting and motivating way to help their pupils engage in literate activities. The task appeared to be meaningful and motivating to the children, providing an authentic audience of peers for their writing.

The role of the teacher

If joint computer-based activities are to be effective in developing students' language skills, teachers need to model and 'scaffold' the development of the kinds of language skills students are expected to use. As illustrated in the teachers' notes previously, this can involve highlighting features of exploratory talk and helping students recognize relevant features of the written genres they are expected to produce (such as feedback comments). In this way, teachers can raise students' awareness of the functional requirements of different types of communication, guiding students' attention towards the intended purposes of their speech and writing, and to the needs of their audiences. An example of a teacher providing this kind of guidance is included as transcript 3 below. As part of their English studies, the members of a class in a secondary school were engaged in an extended computer-based communication with children in a nearby primary school. In a 'fantasy adventure' setting, the secondary students were (in groups of three) pretending to be a group of characters stranded in time and space.

Explanations of their predicaments and requests for solutions were emailed to the primary children, whose responses were considered and developed by each group of students. Transcript 3 is one small part of a recorded session, in which the English teacher is questioning one group of girls (all aged 14) about the most recent interaction and their future plans.

Transcript 3: Dimensions

Teacher: What about the word 'dimension' because you were going to include that in your message, weren't you?
Anne: Yeh. And there's going to be – if they go in the right room, then they'll find a letter in the floor and that'll spell 'dimension'.
Teacher: What happens if they do go in the wrong room?
Emma: Well, there's no letter in the bottom, in the floor.
Teacher: Oh God! So they've got to get it right, or that's it! (*everyone laughs*) For ever. And Cath can't get back to her own time. What

	do you mean the letters are in the room, I don't quite follow that?
Emma:	On the floor, like a tile or something.
Teacher:	Oh I see. Why did you choose the word 'dimension'?
Anne:	Don't know (*the three pupils speak together, looking to each other, seeming uncertain*).
Emma:	It just came up. Just said, you know, 'dimension' and everyone agreed.
Sharon:	Don't know.
Teacher:	Right, because it seemed to fit in with, what, the fantasy flow, flavour?
Sharon:	Yeh.
Teacher:	OK. Why do they go through the maze rather than go back? I mean what motivation do they have for going through it in the first place?
Emma:	Um, I think that it was the king told them that Joe would be in the maze or at the end of the maze, and they didn't go back because of Joe, think it was. I'm not sure about that.
Teacher:	You've really got to sort that out. It's got to be very, very clear.
Anne:	Yeh.
Emma:	Joe went through this secret passage, you see, round the edge. And we couldn't go through there it was like a different door.
Teacher:	OK.
Emma:	Yeh and that was like the only way we could meet Joe.
Teacher:	OK. Do remember that anything that you don't explain adequately, the primary school children are going to pick up on, and so it's got to make sense. Particularly at this end of the project, because they're not going to have much time to reply to your messages.

In this sequence the teacher uses questions to draw out from the students the content of their recent email message, and also some justifications for what they included in it. At one level, she is simply monitoring their activity and assessing the adequacy of their attempt to continue the communication with the younger children. But her questions are not merely being used to assess what they know, they are *part of her teaching*. Like many effective teachers, she is using questions not only to monitor students' activity, but also to guide it. Through questions like 'Why did you choose the word "dimension"?' and 'Why do they go through the maze rather than go back?', she directs their attention to matters requiring more thought and clarification. In much of her talk, and particularly her imperative conclusions ('You've really got to sort that out' and 'Do remember . . .') we can see her 'scaffolding' her students' activities, highlighting important aspects of the literate activity and creating continuities between past, present and future events in the classroom experience of her students.

Characteristics of good computer-based collaborative tasks

Our research has identified three related factors which are important for determining the educational value of joint activities at the computer:

- *The teacher's preparation and structuring of the activity* to create the conditions for educationally effective interaction between computers and learners.
- *The ability of the learners to interact effectively* through talk or online communication, and their understanding that this is a critical aspect of the activity.
- *The design of the software* as a stimulus and frame for joint activity.

When used to stimulate discussion, we have found that the most productive computer-based collaborative activities are likely to have several of the following features:

- Before the activity, the teacher will have raised students' awareness of ways of talking together, and ideally have enabled them to develop their skills in using exploratory talk.
- Students must *have* to talk to complete the activity, rather than conversation being merely an optional or incidental accompaniment.
- The activity should be designed to encourage cooperation, rather than competition, between partners.
- The activity should be demanding enough to 'stretch' students, but be within the limits of their possible achievement.
- Students should begin with a clear, shared understanding of the point and purpose of the activity, including why they are being asked to talk and work together.

Software which is well suited for encouraging productive discussion is likely to offer at least several of the following features:

- Activities will include problems which involve the rational consideration of available information, and which are sufficiently complex to benefit from being analysed through joint reflection and discussion.
- Problems and choices are embedded in a motivating narrative or process.
- A clear purpose for the activity is made evident to participants and is kept in focus throughout.
- On-screen prompts remind participants to talk together and encourage them to make predictions, proposals and reasons explicit.
- Information which can be used for reasoning about decisions is clearly presented on the screen.
- Instructions do not encourage rapid decision-making, competition within the group or serial turn-taking.
- Unless the task is expressly concerned with writing development,

responses should require simple keystroke responses rather than extensive typing (as this tends to damage the pace and continuity of discussion).

Summary and conclusion

At the beginning of this chapter we suggested that computers should not be seen simply as a means for organizing individual learning activities, but rather as cultural tools for focusing and stimulating joint intellectual activity. Computers motivate children and hold their attention. In relation to the English curriculum, computer-based activities can be used not only to help develop speaking and listening but also to encourage children to jointly make sense of texts and learn to use new registers and genres. If computer-based activities draw on suitable software and are carried out on the basis of a shared understanding among members of the class about the nature and functions of language use, they have a distinctive and valuable role in the study of the English curriculum. Moreover, one special feature of computers makes them particularly suitable for stimulating discussion: their potentially infinite patience. A pair or group of children who are 'asked' by a computer to discuss a text, or provide a solution to a problem, can take as long as they like to share their thoughts and decide on their response. Because the computer is a machine, it will wait for the children's response until they are ready to provide it. The computer can also be used to organize the process of joint activity more effectively than a conventional worksheet because software can require the children to provide a response before being allowed to continue, remind them of relevant information and provide feedback on their responses. Learners can be offered optional interactive routes through a narrative or information text. Used in combination with the support and guidance of a teacher, ICT can 'scaffold' children's investigation of a text or problem while allowing them control over the pace of their activity. The powerful combination of computer technology and teacher guidance, can thus provide unique opportunities for the development of children's spoken and written language capabilities.

References

Barnes, D. and Todd, F. (1977) *Communication and Learning in Small Groups*. London: Routledge and Kegan Paul.

Barnes, D. and Todd, F. (1995) *Communication and Learning Revisited*. Portsmouth, NH: Heinemann.

Barton, D. (1994) *Literacy: An Introduction to the Ecology of Written Language*. Oxford: Blackwell.

Dawes, L., Mercer, N. and Wegerif, R. (2000) *Thinking Together: Activities for Teachers and Children at Key Stage 2*. Birmingham: Questions Publishing Co.

DfES (2000) *Superhighway Safety: Safe Use of the Internet*. DfES Publications, PO Box 5050, Sudbury, Suffolk CO10 6ZQ. Available at http://safety.ngfl.gov.uk.

Edwards, D. and Mercer, N. (1987) *Common Knowledge: The Development of Understanding in the Classroom*. London: Methuen/Routledge.

Fernandez, M. (2001) Collaborative writing of hypermedia documents and the social construction of knowledge. Paper presented to the 9th European Conference for Research on Learning and Instruction: Bridging Instruction to Learning, Fribourg, Switzerland.

Fisher, E. (1993) Distinctive features of pupil–pupil classroom talk and their relationship to learning: how discursive exploration might be encouraged, *Language and Education*, 7(4): 239–57.

Heath, S.B. (1983) *Ways with Words: Language, Life and Work in Communities and Classrooms*. Cambridge: Cambridge University Press.

Howe, C., Tolmie, A. and Mackenzie, M. (1996) Computer support for the collaborative learning of physics concepts, in C. O'Malley (ed.) *Computer-Supported Collaborative Learning*. Berlin: Springer-Verlag.

Hoyles, C., Sutherland, R. and Healy, I. (1990) Children talking in computer environments: new insights on the role of discussion in mathematics learning, in K. Durkin and B. Shine (eds) *Language and Mathematics Education*. Milton Keynes: Open University Press.

Light, P. and Littleton, K. (1999) *Social Processes in Children's Learning*. Cambridge: Cambridge University Press.

Littleton, K. and Light, P. (1999) *Learning with Computers: Analysing Productive Interaction*. London: Routledge.

Mercer, N. (1994) The quality of talk in children's joint activity at the computer, *Journal of Computer Assisted Learning*, 10: 24–32.

Mercer, N. (2000) *Words and Minds: How We Use Language to Think Together*. London: Routledge.

Mercer, N., Wegerif, R. and Dawes, L. (1999) Children's talk and the development of reasoning in the classroom, *British Educational Research Journal*, 25(1): 95–111.

Pailliotet, A.W. and Mosenthal, P. (2000) (eds) *Reconceptualizing Literacy in the Media Age*. Stamford, CT: Jai Press Inc.

Rassool, N. (1999) *Literacy for Sustainable Development in the Age of Information*. Clevedon: Multilingual Matters.

Scrimshaw, P. (ed.) (1993) *Language, Classrooms and Computers*. London: Routledge.

Sheeran, Y. and Barnes, D. (1991) *School Writing: Discovering the Ground Rules*. Milton Keynes: Open University Press.

Street, B. (1983) *Literacy in Theory and Practice*. Cambridge: Cambridge University Press.

Street, B. (ed.) (1993) *Cross-Cultural Approaches to Literacy*. Cambridge: Cambridge University Press.

Vygotsky, L.S. (1987) Thinking and speech, in R.W. Riber and A.S. Carton (eds) *The Collected Works of L.S. Vygotsky. Vol. 1: Problems of General Psychology*. New York, NY: Plenum.

Wegerif, R. (1996) Collaborative learning and directive software, *Journal of Computer Assisted Learning*, 12: 22–32.

Wegerif, R. (1997) Factors affecting the quality of children's talk at computers, in R. Wegerif and P. Scrimshaw (eds) *Computers and Talk in the Primary Classroom*. Clevedon: Multilingual Matters.

Wegerif, R. and Scrimshaw, P. (eds) (1997) *Computers and Talk in the Primary Classroom*. Clevedon: Multilingual Matters.

Software

Cochard, S., Jordan, D., Horn, K., Wing, J., Chin, B., Carlson, K., Kelley, J., Figueroa, J., Post, B. and Cochard, J. *SiteCentral*, Version 1.0 (Windows platform). El Cajon, CA: Wagner Publishing, 1999.

eMindMaps, Version 2.0.7 (Windows platform) Sausalito, CA: MindJET LCC, 1999.

Kate's Choice can be downloaded free from the Thinking Together website at http://www.thinkingtogether.org.uk. The site also contains examples of Thinking Together activities, research reports and other resources.

Think.com, Version 1.0 (Windows platform). Redwood Shores, CA: Oracle Corporation, 2001. http://www.think.com.

2

WRITING – AND OTHER LANGUAGE MATTERS

Anthony Adams, Kate Sida-Nicholls and Sue Brindley

We have chosen the above double title after careful deliberation: 'Writing' emphasizes what all the evidence shows: that this is by far the main use of ICT in the English classroom in the form of word processing; 'other language matters', makes clear that in the age of the new technologies it is no longer possible to separate English teaching into the traditional areas of reading, writing, speaking and listening, to which for many years in North America has been added 'viewing'.

This is in spite of the fact that when one of us was on a first visit to the USA in 1966, the 'official' English syllabus was based on what was then called the American equivalent of the medieval trivium: literature, grammar (originally rhetoric) and composition. The experience of the American schools was that the syllabus was well ahead of what was then officially demanded. As against that, however, in England it is still the case that examination syllabuses require the above-mentioned four-way split in the English curriculum, and that is what sets the agenda. The basic argument in this chapter is that as language and the world have changed, so the agenda has to be changed accordingly.

As long ago as 1965 Andrew Wilkinson, then at the University of Birmingham, coined the word 'oracy' as the spoken English equivalent of the well-established concept of literacy, in practice mainly written English in the schools of that time. He argued in an introductory chapter, which has resonance for today, that:

> The term we suggest for general ability in the oral skills is *oracy*; one who has these skills is *orate*, one without them *inorate*. An educated person should be numerate, orate and literate. These are the NOL skills; NOL are to our age what the Three Rs were to the nineteenth century; fundamental objects of educational effort.
>
> (Wilkinson 1965: 14; emphasis in original)

All this was written long before the introduction of the new technologies into schools. It is a major contention of this chapter, however, that spoken language (oracy) and a variety of ranges of literacies (including visual literacy, graphicacy – and computer literacy – computeracy) now come together in what has been a recent development among the traditional fields of writing and reading, including new developments in literature.

We have placed writing at the centre of the chapter because, apart from the reading of books, writing is still the major activity of the English classroom and the one with which ICT is most involved. But there are a number of queries to be raised here. The big question is how word processing is being used: is it being used to enable something users have always done (at least since the nineteenth century) to be done better, or to do something new?

Even the term 'word processing' has its problems. As with so much in the age of the new technologies, we are locked into using old metaphors to try to describe the new ways of working. 'Word processing' suggests a means of tidying up existing text, the computer as an intelligent typewriter, which is what it was of course in the initial stages. The basic argument of this chapter is that, so far as good practice is concerned, learning to write with computers goes far beyond this.

In England and Wales, the National Curriculum places considerable emphasis on the importance of students learning to draft and redraft both 'on paper and on screen', and word processing can help with this. But to what end? We would also add that it is just as important to learn to compose on screen, a process which is rather different from drafting.

Indeed, we have argued for some time (Adams and Brindley 1998) that, in practice, most redrafting is simply a matter of the correction of surface features, with little attention to major changes to substance and text organization. We see little reason to change this view today. It might help both teachers and students, if writers were encouraged to use the 'track changes' facilities. Teachers could use this in responding to students' drafts, though we believe that the final draft should always be the one agreed by the student. The replacement of the red pen by the word processor, as a medium for collaboration between teacher and student, seems something to be in need of urgent exploration (Graves 1981).

In any case, the concept of drafting suggests a single model for writing which is certainly subject to change. One of us recalls that, when at school, he was required to provide an 'essay plan' for the essays he wrote. He interpreted this by writing the essay first and the plan afterwards.

Chandler (1995) makes a useful distinction. He says:

> Some individuals seem to exhibit a fairly consistent need to revise more than others do . . . This can be interpreted in terms of a continuum, at the poles of which are: *Discoverers*, who write to 'discover' what they want to say, typically planning minimally and revising extensively; and *Planners*, who write primarily to record or communicate their ideas, typically planning extensively, executing the plan and revising relatively minimally.
>
> (Chandler 1995: 60; emphasis in original)

One should add that, for some writers, the 'planning' process may be conducted in the head so that they know exactly what they want to write before sitting down in front of a sheet of paper or the keyboard. The other real danger, in the case of the Discoverers, is how they ever reach closure – they can go on revising for ever. With these writers, the penultimate draft is always the last draft, until the next one. How to reach closure remains a serious problem for such writers. The British poet Simon Armitage is reported as saying that his poems are never finished, just aborted.

The crucial thing is to recognize that different students compose in different ways and not always consistently. To enable this differentiation seems important from the teaching point of view. In some cases the use of the computer simply as a medium for the correction of surface features may be more justified. However, even here, some notes of caution are advisable. Students need to be taught explicitly how to use such tools as spell and grammar (more effectively style) checkers. Unthinking use of these can lead to more errors than those corrected. It is important to ask oneself whether Microsoft English is not fast becoming a new and virtually universal dialect of English. The basic point is to recognize individual differences in the ways in which people apply themselves to the process of composition and that (when working as individuals) they will use word processing in different ways.

However, we argue that there are more significant ways of using computers in the writing classroom. Some of these ways were devised by our late colleague, Stephen Marcus, of the University of Santa Barbara in California (Chandler and Marcus 1985) who conducted some interesting experiments (which we have replicated) with what he called invisible writing. There were two version of this, both of which we would recommend. In the first, students were encouraged to write at a word processor with their screen switched off, thus enabling them to concentrate on the content and deal with the surface feature 'corrections' at a later stage.

In the second version, which we have found particularly powerful, students work in pairs but each has a screen that is linked to the other's keyboard. Student A begins a composition which is visible only on Student B's screen. Student B then feeds back constructive comments which appear on Student A's screen, while the composing process is in progress. Again it is important that the concern here is not with surface features but with content, such as 'Tell me more about . . .' or 'What do you mean by . . .?'

One of our colleagues (Russell King, personal communication, 2005) opines that the use, in the first version, of invisible writing is common practice in schools which have a strong English and ICT programme. King also argues that it is valuable for teachers to design positive tasks for students about the redrafting process. For example, writing for a new audience, altering tenses and redrafting poetry from narrative into imagist forms.

The notion of drafting goes back to the late 1970s in North America when there was much emphasis on involving professional writers in school education, notably Donald Murray, with the concept of learning 'to write like a reader' (Murray 1978, 1980). Such ideas were quickly taken up by educationists, such as Frank Smith (1983, 1988) and Donald Graves (1981). Both of these influential writers, placed great importance on the idea of creating a community of writers within the classroom. In fact 'collaborative writing' was very much part of the new agenda, not however without some criticisms from those engaged in conventional schooling, as Smith vividly admits:

> One of the most unpopular assignments I ever set graduate students in colleges of education, was to work together on projects on which they would share the labour and the grade . . . The students gave three main reasons why they would prefer not to work together: (1) group work would lead to disputes and lower the quality of the products, (2) somehow all individuals would be trapped into doing more work than their collaborators, and (3) individuals would not get credit for their good ideas, which might in fact be 'stolen'. In other words, graduate students regarded working in collaboration as less efficient and less rewarding than working alone. Where would anyone learn to look upon collaboration in such a negative way? Where in fact could collaboration be an undesirable activity? The answer, obviously, is in school. Remember, my graduate students were all experienced teachers.
>
> And indeed, I got exactly the same response when second-grade children were encouraged to collaborate on assignments. If the assignment was not to be graded the six-year-olds did not think it worth doing at all, and if it carried a mark they preferred to do it by themselves. Many children (unlike the adults) said that working together was 'cheating' . . . But what the children were in fact demonstrating was what they had

been taught in school – that learning is essentially a solitary and competitive matter.

(Smith 1988: 69)

Unfortunately, this attitude is still all too prevalent in schools today. The examination system itself places a huge premium on students' individual work. An experienced senior examiner colleague of ours argued, when still a classroom teacher, against the recent emphasis on drafting on the grounds that in the examination room there was no time for students to draft and redraft in a traditional three-hour paper.

Similarly, at doctoral level, candidates have to sign a declaration that the thesis is their 'own unaided work'. There is much concern at present over issues of plagiarism given the wide availability of access to the Internet.

However, such concerns may be locked into a print-based model of writing and composition. Even the term 'copyright' suggests the world of print, and it is worth noting that it derives from the beginnings of the print age and was essentially a means of enforcing censorship in the Elizabethan era, when texts had to be registered at the Stationers' Company.

Our contention is that all this is rooted in a nineteenth-century model of schooling and fails to take cognizance of the revolutionary effect of the new technologies on language which, properly used, provide much more potential for effective collaborative work. This is, after all, the kind of work usually needed in the workplace.

We therefore query whether, in the twenty-first century, a model of writing that is locked into the twentieth (if not the nineteenth) century is the best practical, and the most effective, use of what is still a relatively scarce resource in the English classroom.

We say 'English classroom' deliberately as, still too often in schools, the computers are housed in specific computer laboratories which have to be booked, often many weeks in advance: a situation which makes them pretty useless for effective English work when they need to be available on the spot, as and when they need to be used.

We have seen some very effective new school developments on English and/or humanities suites with a bank of networked computers, but this is hardly a practical suggestion except in specially designed new schools. Since we advocate group work as a basis for the use of computers in the classroom and our experience suggests that three students to a computer is ideal, one relatively economic solution is the use of laptops, ten of which would be needed for a class of thirty students. However, since laptops are easily portable, one such set can serve several classes within the English department. The addition of at least one, or preferably two, Internet access points in each classroom and a portable data-projector, enables computer power to become much more immediately available to the English department as a whole. The potential of wireless networking also needs further exploration as the cost of such technology is rapidly decreasing. We have seen some very interesting work in a Canadian high school where all the students had their own laptops with wireless connectivity. Groups of students were working in different areas of the classrooms but working together on a project which, in this case, was the evaluation of other schools' websites, together with a detailed evaluation report.

There is also the added advantage that most secondary students will have access to computers at home and can bring their work to school to share with their peers and teachers, and expand the cause of collaborative learning and writing. (In practice, much collaboration between students takes place out of school hours, through the use of the Internet, far more than most teachers would think.) It goes without saying that individual teachers need their own laptop and Internet access at home so that they, too, can be involved in the collaborative process. Departmental budgets should allow for this as a high priority.

There are other alternatives. One, much vaunted at the time of writing by the British government, is the use of interactive whiteboards in the classroom. The following case study by a schoolteacher colleague, Kate Sida-Nicholls, developed through her work at the King Edward VI School in Suffolk, demonstrates how these whiteboards can be used in the writing process.

Using the interactive whiteboard in the classroom

By the term 'interactive whiteboard' I mean a large, touch-sensitive whiteboard connected to a digital projector and a computer. The screen of the computer is projected onto this whiteboard and, either by using a special pen or even fingers, images and text can be manipulated without having to go near the computer. There are various software packages that come with the interactive whiteboard, and the one chosen will dictate the special effects that you can create. Most software packages will allow you to use a special pen to write directly on the screen; others will allow you to hide text, reveal text, darken the screen, and to colour the screen and text. If using an interactive whiteboard, you should ensure the software is loaded not only onto the computer in the classroom but also onto the computer usually used for the preparation of school work.

Whichever method is used to display your data, prepare to spend time on the preparation. It takes time to find resources on the Internet, create PowerPoint presentations, and create files that allow students to interact with data. On the other hand, it can all be saved for use in future lessons and, with access to a printer, it can be printed out for students who have missed lessons or for students to add to their own notes. I resent less the time spent preparing lessons using the interactive whiteboard than the necessity to wipe off from a traditional whiteboard all my well-prepared notes at the end of a lesson.

Effective use of ICT in the classroom can only be achieved when a combination of factors has taken place: teachers need to be confident with the ICT equipment and they need to have easy access to the equipment; students need to be engaged with the task and forward planning needs to take place. All of these aspects are essential in order to produce an effective lesson using ICT.

The interactive whiteboard requires teachers to move away from simply giving instructions about the operation of computers and developing students' word processing skills. In order for the interactive whiteboard to work successfully in the classroom, the pedagogical role of a teacher has to change. Teachers need to view the interactive whiteboard as a tool that develops and extends their current teaching methods. Effective use is not just as a 'trendy' way of displaying existing material, such as presenting current material using PowerPoint slides. There should be recognition of its educational value in the classroom and how it can be used to develop specific skills of group work, discussion, critical analysis and learning styles.

The British Educational Communications and Technology Agency (Becta) has recently been conducting research on the use of ICT in the classroom, together with the use of interactive whiteboards. A couple of completed studies and some briefing papers about the progress of current research can be found on its website at www.becta.org.uk. One study commissioned by Becta on behalf of the Department for Education and Skills (DfES) and conducted by a research team at King's College, London, investigated the effects of ICT pedagogy on attainment (Cox *et al.* 2003). The study was based on evidence from the published research literature and a small set of case studies in schools, identified for their advanced and/or integrated uses of ICT. Cox *et al.* state that the pedagogical roles of teachers have to alter in a classroom using ICT. They use an example from McLoughlin and Oliver (1999) who define pedagogical roles for teachers in a technology-supported classroom: as including setting joint tasks, rotating roles, promoting student self-management, supporting meta-cognition, fostering multiple perspectives and scaffolding learning.

The teacher needs to move away from simply using the interactive whiteboard for its 'wow' factor. Instead there is a need to think about how it changes the pedagogical approach to teaching. Our pedagogical knowledge (that is to say our knowledge about teaching methods, teaching objectives and classroom management combined with our subject knowledge) needs to change when using ICT. We need to think about how the material can be delivered to develop specific skills rather than just focus on the content and the entertainment factor of using the Internet or colourful images.

In an article entitled 'Something old, something new: Is pedagogy affected by ICT?', Loveless, *et al.* (2001: 70) point out that, as teachers, we should use ICT:

to model and reflect the very concepts on which pedagogical content knowledge needs to draw – using the speed, automatic functions, capacity, range, provisionality and interactivity of ICT to support capability in researching information, developing ideas and trying these out, exchanging and sharing information and critically reflecting on the quality of the process of developing knowledge from a variety of sources of information.

The use of the interactive whiteboard in this manner allows teachers to shift the focus away from the students' development of basic keyboard skills and onto the wider skills that are encouraged in all subjects.

The research from the report by Cox *et al.* (2003) supports this move away from seeing ICT as a tool simply to develop presentational or comprehension skills. The report states:

> studies show that the most effective uses of ICT are those in which the teacher and the software can challenge pupils' understanding and thinking, either through whole-class discussions using an interactive whiteboard or through individual or paired work on a computer. If the teacher has the skills to organize and stimulate the ICT-based activity, then both whole-class and individual work can be equally effective.
>
> (Cox *et al.* 2003: 4)

In my experience many teachers shy away from using ICT in this kind of interactive manner in their classroom due to lack of opportunity, resources and time. However, there is growing evidence that it is essential to build teachers' confidence in this area as it will result in ICT proving to be an asset to learning and teaching, rather than simply acting as a presentational tool.

In England, the National Strategy requires English teachers to use various effective teaching styles: direction, demonstration, modelling, scaffolding, explanation, questioning, exploration and investigation. What follows is a look at these teaching styles to show how they can be incorporated into lessons using an interactive whiteboard.

As far as indicating the direction of the lesson, I find that using the interactive whiteboard simply as an extension of a computer screen can be an effective teaching tool as the image on my screen is projected onto the wall. I type onto the screen either the learning objectives of the lesson, three questions that I would like answered, a summary of yesterday's lesson or a visual image that is connected to the topic of the current lesson. This takes little time if there is a standard document already saved onto the computer, which can be prepared as you plan your lesson. I find this an effective tool for focusing the lesson and students' attention. Typing out key questions to be answered, by some point in the lesson, is very useful because these questions can be saved and used again in future lessons. This is much less labour intensive than writing them out on a traditional whiteboard and having to wipe them off each time.

A computer that is linked to the Internet, with either a projector or an interactive whiteboard, is very useful when teaching demonstration or modelling. I use the interactive whiteboard for demonstrating short grammar activities that can form the beginning section of a lesson.

The following is typical of a starting activity about simple and complex sentences that is sometimes used. Students take it in turn to come up to the board and move the boxes around. Once the students get used to working with the interactive whiteboard they quickly form the habit of choosing the next person to come up and work with the board. They will quite happily pass the pen to someone else in the room. Sometimes I intervene in the selection process, and tell them that I want the next student to come to the front to be a boy or a girl or someone they do not talk to normally, but usually they tend to adopt their own successful strategy.

This sort of demonstration activity can be used on an interactive whiteboard, or on a laptop with a projector, and the students can use a mouse to manipulate the text boxes. With access to an infra-red keyboard which can be passed round the room, this activity can be extended by the students adding their own clauses for others to complete. Using the software that comes with an interactive whiteboard, demonstration activities like the one above can be made more dynamic because you can hide text boxes, darken the screen, reveal answers, include images and use the pen to write on the screen.

For modelling and explanation activities, I tend to use the interactive whiteboard for PowerPoint presentations. I find extracts of various texts from the Internet and save them into PowerPoint and then we discuss the features of the texts that are relevant to the objectives of the lesson.

The use of the interactive whiteboard enables the inclusion of examples of texts that are modern and topical that will capture students' interest. For example, by using a computer that is connected to the Internet you can download from various websites a topical news story and, through various strategies of class discussions, group work and questioning, collaboratively demonstrate whether it is a good example of a piece of non-fiction writing. The students do not need to have their own computers for this sort of exercise: one screen projecting onto a wall through an interactive whiteboard, or a laptop with a projector, is sufficient.

For scaffolding activities the interactive whiteboard can act as an extension of what the students may have in front of them on their desks. I may give students a series of headings, words, topics or phrases, and then ask them to structure these ideas, through the use of the whiteboard, into a piece of writing. Students may come up to the whiteboard and write on the screen themselves, or I may have images or examples that scaffold the piece of writing that we are aiming for. This way the students feel ownership for the piece of writing or activity, and we are working collaboratively. They enjoy the act of manipulating data on the big screen rather than perhaps the traditional technique of moving cards round the desk.

I have found the most successful ways to develop the skills of investigation and exploration is through the use of digital video editing. The interactive whiteboard or a computer linked to a video with a projector, is a very effective tool for this exercise. In the first instance the students are looking at a giant screen which they find entertaining. Becta has issued advice for teachers on using ICT (see www.ictadvice.org.uk). In these documents, Becta outlines the various skills and tasks that can be developed using digital video. Using the large screen it is possible to engage the whole class in analysing extracts of films, videos, trailers, adverts and so on. Some of these can be downloaded directly from the Internet, whereas others can be looked at by connecting a standard video or DVD player to a laptop. With this exercise you are not only giving students the relevant vocabulary but also teaching them the key skills of critical evaluation, reflection, discussion and teamwork. All of these skills have wide applications beyond the English classroom.

To provide a specific example, my class has on many occasions looked at various film versions of a Shakespeare play. We do not look at the complete films but concentrate on specific scenes that are either relevant as a set scene, at age 13, or required for coursework or examination essay. Software is available that allows the editing of various scenes together, and by using your computer you can transmit a seamless series of clips for the class to evaluate and explore. Alternatively, you can simply load in videos or DVDs in the correct order and change them over manually at the end of each task. I am always pleased how eagerly my students respond to the task but I am also astonished at how complicit students are at taking one film's interpretation as the established one. As far as they are concerned, because a film has been made its interpretation is necessarily correct and should not be criticized. The characters, setting and language are all accepted because they are being viewed on the 'big screen'. We have endless debates about the merits of an individual's imagination, influence of directors, effect of presentational devices and use of digital technology in films.

A main benefit of using an interactive whiteboard is that it takes away the need to concentrate on the operation of the equipment. Too often, when using computers with students, we are distracted from the main objectives of the lesson as we get involved in dealing with students who cannot access their password or follow instructions. By contrast, the interactive whiteboard allows the teacher to engage with the students and develop their skills from the opportunities that have been created.

It is this pedagogical shift that has to occur to enable teachers to develop a more widespread use of interactive whiteboards in the classroom.

When planning a lesson using an interactive whiteboard, the same considerations of planning as in other lessons need to be made: that is, the lesson's objectives and its outcomes need to be thought about. Neither of these should be the improvement of the students' ICT skills. The lesson should be focused purely on the development of skills that we need to study the subject of English. A good analogy to develop this point is the use of overhead projectors in the classroom. Teachers regularly use overhead projectors to present material on transparencies. We do not expect the students to be impressed with our skills in using the projector; in fact we do not want them to be aware of it as a piece of equipment. Instead, we want the students to engage and interact with the material that is being presented to them. We need to take the same approach to using interactive whiteboards in the classroom. The technological effects that can be created using the interactive whiteboards can be used to enhance the dynamism of the lesson, but should not take over the purpose of the lesson.

Too often I have seen teachers standing back after using the interactive whiteboard with a smile on their face because the students seem more engaged with a task now than when it had been taught in the traditional way. However, analysis of the task shows that it is usually asking the students to perform exactly the same activities as on previous occasions. This is disappointing, as using the interactive whiteboard in this manner misses the opportunities that teachers can give to students to see ICT in the classroom as a valuable teaching tool that focuses on critical analysis, and instead develops a simple compliant response to its presentational features.

Interactive whiteboards are not cheap but I think their value for money can be justified as long as teachers are prepared to embark on a pedagogical shift of their teaching when using them in the classroom. I have found their use to be extremely rewarding and hope this case study will inspire you to feel more confident about incorporating their use into your own classroom.

Given, through whatever means, the availability of access to the necessary hardware in the classroom we need to ask whether there are potentially new and different approaches that will bring the teaching of writing with ICT support into the twenty-first century. The main obstacle to this remains the nineteenth-century model of schooling. In England and Wales, the domination of the National Literacy Strategy remains supreme and has failed to recognize the impact that ICT has had on writing. This (the official view) is strongly reinforced by the Key Stage 3 (11–14-year-old students) Framework (KS3F) in England and Wales which reads as follows in relation to writing:

By the end of Year 9, we expect each pupil to be:
• A confident writer.
• Able to write for a variety of purposes and audiences.
• Able to write imaginatively, effectively and correctly.
• Able to shape, express, experiment with and manipulate sentences.
• Able to organize, develop, spell and punctuate writing accurately.

(DfEE 2001)

The model of writing, presented here, is not necessarily one which we would want to argue against; but we would want to argue that, as it stands, it is inadequate.

The first thing to recognize is that the notion of the individual writer, as embedded in the Framework document, was largely the consequence of the invention of printing. Before that, most writing was essentially collaborative (including, probably, many of the plays of Shakespeare, who rarely invented a plot and never acknowledged his sources). Many other earlier eminent writers, the Venerable Bede for example, 'borrowed' from other writers in the field quite freely without quoting any references. As T.S. Eliot once wrote (and who could know better): 'Immature poets imitate; mature poets steal.'

With the advent of the new technologies, we are arguably in a post-print age, accompanied by a need to return to more collaborative models of writing. An example of this is how this chapter was itself composed. It started as classroom work by ourselves and our students (to which we return with practical examples later), followed by brainstorming, discussion and research. Further talk led to scribbles, which then emerged into a first draft, followed by further discussion between ourselves and our collaborative writers leading to many successive drafts.[1]

More discussions followed, leading to the final draft, itself followed by technical discussion about production with the publishers. All of this took much longer than the conventional process without ICT (though, hopefully, this resulted in a better product), but would have been quite impossible without the resources of email and computers.

It is also worth mentioning that different parts of this chapter were written at different times, by no means sequentially. It might therefore be more appropriate to say that the chapter has been 'assembled' rather than 'written'. This points to possible ways of helping school students to use computers in their own composition work.

The impact of email and texting on the language and upon the process of composition cannot be stressed too strongly. There is a good academic study of this in Crystal (2001) who claims that 'netspeak is a radically new linguistic medium. Like it or loathe it, we cannot ignore it.' In this chapter we are more concerned with its practical implications for the secondary classroom. However, an obvious and important point is that the informal style of email makes it in many ways more like speaking than writing. The traditional boundaries in language teaching are being fundamentally broken down. This does raise cultural conflicts both across generations and across nationalities, well exemplified by an email to one of us recently from a colleague in Japan which began: 'Hi! Dear Sir . . .'. One of our tasks as English teachers is to help students understand the various registers involved and for us, too, to understand the shifting registers that are fundamental to the present developments of English as a world language, especially as, for the time being at least, English is the lingua franca on the Internet.

It is a fact of life that most secondary school students will have a mobile phone. The latest generation (at the time of writing) will also incorporate a digital camera and have email and Internet access. Much communication between, or among, students will take place through texting, both within the classroom (often clandestine) or outside it. One of our consultants (an English teacher) on this chapter responded to an earlier comment: 'Me, 2.' The big question is, following Crystal, whether we 'like it or loathe it' how do we as English teachers respond to it.

As long ago as 1988, in the Kingman Report on the teaching of the English language, this was foreshadowed:

> Round the city of Caxton, the electronic suburbs are rising. To the language of books is added the language of television and radio, the elliptical demotic of the telephone, the processed codes of the computer. As the shapes of literacy multiply, so our dependence on language increases. But if language motivates change, it is itself changed. To understand the principles on which that change takes place should be denied to no one.
>
> (DES 1988: 2.7)

We quoted this in our introduction to Monteith (2005), but repeat it here. The issue is whether the English teacher attempts to resist these changes or encourages and capitalizes upon them.

Our view, quite unequivocally, is that these new developments in the language should be both embraced and celebrated. One very interesting development has been that, for several years, the *Guardian* newspaper has run a text poem competition for schools. The winning entry in the first year, together with many other examples and comments from the judges, can be found at the *Guardian Unlimited* website (http://guardian.co.uk/textpoetry) which is strongly recommended.

This seems a very creative use of language and a new approach to writing. But it may not be so new. After all, in our younger days as teachers, we encouraged students to write 'telegrams' or *haikus*, essentially exercises in using language economically. Telegrams did exist in those days, so learning how to write them was important. In the same way, texting now exists, although we suspect that many students could teach their teachers more about this linguistic development than the other way round.

As with telegrams in the past, text messages have their own conventions about the use of language in terms if the number of characters allowed: 160 in all cases, which includes spaces between words. This explains the use of abbreviations and the mixture of text forms, such as the use of numerics alongside conventional text.

Traditionalists have attacked these developments as destroying the language and leading to illiteracy. However, a major research project conducted over twenty-five years by Alf Massey of the University of Cambridge, as reported in *The Times* (31 October 2005), claims that 'today's teenagers are using far more complex sentence structures, wider vocabulary and a more accurate use of capital letters, punctuation and spelling'. The headline reads: 'Texting teenagers are proving more literate than ever before.'

This is supported by a recent statement by the government's advisory group on the curriculum and assessment in England and Wales, the Qualifications and Curriculum Authority (QCA), as reported in *The Times* of 13 October 2005. In *Meeting the Challenge* (2005), the QCA states that English classes must change to reflect the impact of technology on the way people speak and write. The QCA goes on to say, that while books were 'not defunct', children would need 'new literacy skills' to cope with the effect of technology on English in everyday life. It went on to say that it would be 'entering dialogues on curriculum moderization' with teachers, parents and employers in the coming months.

An interesting example of this was reported in the *Guardian* (3 May 2001):

A church in Hanover, Germany, has found a new way of spreading the message. This afternoon it will relay part of its service by text message (SMS) to anyone who has registered on their website.

One of the problems it has had to overcome is reducing the *325* characters in the Our Father prayer to the *160* permitted in a text message. (emphasis in original)

This, incidentally, seems to us to have serious theological as well as linguistic implications.

Once the potential of visual and video material is added to text and email messages (now commonplace), it becomes clear that the traditional division into writing, reading, listening and talking, makes no sense in the English curriculum of the twenty-first century.

Brindley *et al.*, in their discussion of text mapping (Chapter 3, this book), also show clearly that reading and writing can reinforce each other. In this way the notion of English teaching as a seamless whole (which many English teachers have always recognized) becomes a clear reality.

Conventional publishers have been slow to respond to these new developments in writing but already printed texts are showing the impact of the new technologies. For example, the use of bullet points is now commonplace as is the use of section headings. The series to which this book belongs is a good example of this, if compared with earlier Open University Press books with which we have been associated. There is no doubt that this is a trend that will continue and it is difficult to conceive what the printed word, if it exists, will look like in twenty-five years time. Dobson (Chapter 6) looks at the development and impact of electronic text, and there is no doubt that this is an area that is expanding. It is generally agreed that most publishing in the not-too-distant future will be in electronic form, certainly in the case of journals, and this will have its impact on the printed word as well. For fuller discussion of this see Tweddle *et al.* (1997).

There is a sense in which writers have always struggled to get beyond the linear limitations of print. We can go back to George Herbert's experiments with what we would now call graphics, in printed form ('Easter Wings' and 'The Altar' for example); to Lewis Carroll's 'The Mouse's Tale' and Edwin Morgan's 'Message Clear' as well as, in prose, Laurence Sterne's *Tristram Shandy* and James Joyce's *Ulysses*, to which we could add many other examples.

There were also, in the 1960s and 1970s, some interesting experiments in print form with non-linear text, such as Alan Sharp's *Story Trails*, branching stories published by Cambridge University Press, or stories with alternative endings, such as John Fowles' *The French Lieutenant's Woman* (1969), both of which were clearly, directly or indirectly, influenced by the new technologies.

There is a very real sense in which there has always been creative tension between writers and publishers, at least since the invention of the printed word. An obvious, though important, example of this is William Blake, who had to invent his techniques of engraving to enable him to present his 'visions' in print. Likewise, most of Dickens' novels took their form, and their genius, from periodical publication. Additionally, of course, Dickens' own sense and experience of theatre led to the dramatic quality of much of his text.

Even with this book we have felt the constraints of conventional publication. We would have liked for example, to be able to use much more in the way of variable fonts and font sizes, and especially, colour printing, for which some of the chapters cry out. The real problem, as we suggest above, is that writers are always wanting to break beyond the boundaries of the linear text, whereas publishers need, largely for economic reasons, to have a 'house style' to which the text has to conform.

Kress (1995) has argued that all text is essentially multimedia, in that decisions have to be made about fonts, layout, the use of white space and so on. He goes on to claim that, even in schools, informational texts have predominately visual format, with ideas conveyed through pictures. No longer are illustrations a mere accompaniment to the exploration of a concept given through words; pictures have become the basic vehicle for explanatory text. The difference is that with the advent of desktop publishing, the potential for putting more of the control of this into the hands of the author becomes possible.

In this context we would, in particular, mention the graphic novel, a form taken much more seriously in many other countries than in the UK. But here its potential has created at least one major writer/illustrator, Raymond Briggs, who among others has shown the graphic novel's adaptability to tragedy and satire as well as being the format for a favourite children's book (see, for example, *When the Wind Blows, The Iron Lady and the Tinpot Foreign General* and *The Snowman*).

An Australian colleague of ours has edited two very interesting and thought-provoking books on teaching literary theory through picture books. (Stephens and Watson 1994; Watson 1997). Interesting developments in the present and last centuries are represented by the surrealist approach to literature, such as a 'novel' printed on separate cards and presented in a box, recently reprinted. The 'reader' threw the cards into the air and picked them up in any order to construct the 'novel' that was being read. In a sense the whole development of reader-response theory of literary criticism encapsulates this in more academic terms.

All this goes back as long as the Dada movement of 1916 with the work of Tristan Tzara who developed the idea of 'cut ups', poems made out of random phrases and assembled in no particular order except by chance. The most recent example of this technique (of which we are aware) is by Rawle (2005), who used cut up material from women's magazines to produce a complex 'assembled' novel.

Thus, the distinction between writer and reader breaks down. The 'text', as Rosenblatt (1978) argues, is essentially the result of collaboration between the writer and the reader. There is a sense in which we can never read the same text twice; each subsequent reading will be affected by earlier readings and, hopefully, by discussion with other readers.

All this points to a model of English teaching which is essentially collaborative in its style of teaching and learning and which has been further facilitated by the new technologies. For example, one of us worked for several years at a major agricultural show in the East of England, with a group of trainee teachers and school students, producing a daily showground news-sheet. In the first year this consisted of a back page for a professionally-produced free newspaper, of a somewhat conventional kind, with the students writing poems. As the project developed over the years, it changed dramatically. In its final year the students were producing a daily newspaper, a broadsheet poster and an associated website, giving up-to-date news of the latest showground events of the day. They also interviewed and responded in print and visuals to many high-profile visitors to the show. Most of this time the 'teachers', while still acting as advisers, were reduced to the role of amanuenses, doing the day-to-day typing and handing over the real work to the students, working as a collaborative ensemble.

This seems a sound model for future in and out of the classroom activity.

But, most importantly, as we have argued elsewhere (Adams and Brindley 1998), the added-value of the electronic age is that this collaboration is no longer limited in time or space. It is now possible for students working in different countries to collaborate together and to share their insights, cultures and experiences. Within Europe, a lot of valuable work has been established by the European School Net (http://www.eun.org/portal/index.htm).

It seems appropriate to conclude this chapter with a reference to Lewis Carroll, himself a major textual innovator, who, in the following two quotations from *Alice in Wonderland*, neatly encapsulates the two views of the written text we have been exploring. The first, represents the traditional linear view of text:

'Begin at the beginning,' the King said gravely, 'and go on till you come to the end: then stop.'

(Carroll 1865: Chapter 12)

The second is representative of the more dynamic version of text we have argued for in this chapter:

'What is the use of a book,' thought Alice, 'without pictures or conversation?'

(Carroll 1865: Chapter 1).

As always, Alice shows herself to be more aware than the adults who surround and patronize her.

Finally, we might note that the word 'text' itself originally derives from the same root as 'textile'. A text is literally something 'woven' and this is something enabled by the word processor to an extent that the age of print could never contemplate.

Note

1. In this connection we are especially indebted to a former Cambridge student of ours, Russell King, currently Head of Lower School and Media Studies at Passmores School and Technology College, Harlow, Essex, for his insightful comments on various earlier drafts of this chapter.

References

Adams, A. and Brindley, S. (1998) Information technology and collaborative writing, *Journal of Information Technology and Initial Teacher Education*, 7(2).

Carroll, L. (1865) Alice in Wonderland, in M. Gardner (ed.) (2001) *The Annotated Alice*. London: Penguin Books.

Chandler, D. (1995) *The Act of Writing*. Aberystwyth: University of Wales.

Chandler, D. and Marcus, S. (1985) *Computers and Literacy*. Milton Keynes: Open University Press.

Cox, M., Webb, M., Abbott, C., Blakeley, B., Beauchamp, T. and Rhodes, V. (eds) (2003) *ICT and Pedagogy*, Schools Research and Evaluation Series no. 18. Coventry: Becta.

Crystal, D. (2001) *Language and the Internet*. Cambridge: Cambridge University Press.

DES (1988) *Report of the Committee of Inquiry into the Teaching of the English Language* (The Kingman Report). London: HMSO.

DfEE (2001) *Key Stage 3 National Strategy Framework for Teaching English: Years 7, 8 and 9*.

Graves, D. (1981) *Donald Graves in Australia*, Rozelle, NSW: Primary English Teaching Association.

Kress, G. (1995) *Writing the Future: English and the Making of a Culture of Innovation*. Sheffield: NATE.

Loveless, A., Devoogd, G. and Bohlin, R. (2001) Something old, something new: Is pedagogy affected by ICT?, in A. Loveless and V. Ellis (eds) *ICT, Pedagogy and the Curriculum*. London: RoutledgeFalmer.

McLoughlin, C. and Oliver, R. (1999) Pedagogic roles and dynamics in telematics environments, in M. Selinger and J. Pearson (eds) *Telematics in Education: Trends and Issues*. Oxford: Elsevier Science.

Monteith, M. (ed.) (2005) *Teaching Secondary School Literacies with ICT*. Maidenhead: Open University Press.

Murray, D.K (1978) Internal revision – a process of discovery, in C.R. Cooper and L. Odell (eds) *Research on Computing*. Urbana, IL: NCTE.

Murray, D.K (1980) The feel of writing – and teaching writing, in A. Freedman and I. Pringle (eds) *Reinventing the Rhetorical Tradition*. Conway, AK: Canadian Council of Teachers of English/L&S Books.

QCA (2005) *Meeting the Challenge*. London: HMSO.

Rawle, G. (2005) *Woman's World*. London: Atlantic Books.

Rosenblatt, L. (1978) *The Reader, The Text, The Poem: The Transactional Theory of the Literary Work*. Carbondale: Southern Illinois University Press.

Smith, F. (1983) *Essays into Literacy*. Exeter, NH: Heinemann.

Smith, F. (1988) *Joining the Literacy Club*. Portsmouth, NH: Heinemann.

Stephens, J. and Watson, K. (eds) (1994) *From Picture Books to Literary Theory*. Sydney: St Clair Press.

Tweddle, S., Adams, A., Clarke, S., Scrimshaw, P. and Walton, S. (1997) *English for Tomorrow*. Buckingham: Open University Press.

Watson, K. (ed.) (1997) *Word and Image*. Sydney: St Clair Press.

Wilkinson, A. (1965) Spoken English, *Educational Review* (University of Birmingham), 17(2).

3

MODELS OF READING IN THE SECONDARY CLASSROOM: LITERATURE AND BEYOND

Sue Brindley, David Greenwood and Anthony Adams

If the 'e' in e-learning can be said to stand for enhanced, the teaching of literature may be a good place to begin exploring the impact of ICT on the English classroom. Literature has long been the centre of the English classroom; an exploration of opportunities for an expansion of the strategies that underpin the teaching of literature and the traditional skills of literary analysis which accompany these, through an examination of current classroom practice using ICT will, it is hoped, contribute positively to the notion of enhancement.

It is our contention that ICT changes both the construction of text and the act of reading. In this chapter, we want to propose that secondary classroom reading should be understood in three major ways in relation to ICT. These are not thought to be exclusive, but to perhaps contribute to the debates which have existed, and no doubt will continue to exist, about reading in the secondary English classroom.

First, we want to consider the ways in which ICT can be said to enhance the activity of reading what we might consider to be 'classic texts' – that is, those texts which make up the staple diet of many secondary English classrooms. These might be understood, though this list is indicative, not exhaustive, to consist of Key Stage 3 (students aged 11–14) 'preferred texts' such as those by David Almond, Jacqueline Wilson and Philip Pullman, the poetry of Carol Ann Duffy and Simon Armitage, and selected pre-twentieth-century poets such as Alfred, Lord Tennyson (for example, *The Lady of Shalott*); and for Key Stage 4 (students aged 14–16) and A level (post-16) those texts which constitute the texts of examination syllabuses, such as Steinbeck's *Of Mice and Men*, J.B. Priestley's *An Inspector Calls* and the poetry of Tony Harrison, Seamus Heaney, John Agard, Monica Alvi and Derek Walcott.

Second, we want to consider the reading of electronic texts and the ways in which (and the extent to which) the text form, for example the place of graphics and the physical representation of text beyond the linear, make different demands on the reader.

Third, we want to consider how text and provisionality, for example the reading of wikipedias, have brought an additional dimension to the notion of reader-response theory – the demise of the concept of closure in relation to the construction of text and the ways in which this concept can enhance the notion of drafting written text.

As part of our thinking about these areas, we have drawn heavily on classroom practices of a number of colleagues whose work (generously shared with us) has both stimulated our thinking and provided a rich source of case study materials, represented in this chapter.[1]

Classic texts

The secondary English classroom has its roots in a vision of English as a place concerned with values and beliefs, meaning and interpretation, and the classroom text is where the exploration of these dimensions has led to a wealth of innovative practice in the English classroom (much of this practice now forming the basis for the pedagogical recommendations for teachers across the curriculum in the Key Stage 3 Framework; DfEE 2001).

The claims that English has 'no content' are ill founded. The entire canon of world literatures is enough of a content base for any subject, we would have thought. But what is unique about English is that reading the text is unlikely to be the sole focus of any English lesson: the text is the medium for teaching critical engagement with ideas – the ideas contained within the text.

Ways of accessing ideas and of bringing that understanding to interpretation of literary texts – and of bringing about critical engagement with those ideas – is therefore a key activity for English teachers. We already have a number of well-established approaches: indeed Cox (1991) lists over thirty in the annex to the National Curriculum. They will be familiar to many of us: exploring character and motivation through hot seating;

decentring the text to bring about understanding of plurality of perspective; teaching texts in parallel to demonstrate the handling of ideas (for example, Attwood's *The Handmaid's Tale* with Huxley's *Brave New World*). Drawing on the social constructivist positioning of English shared by many (though by no means all) English teachers, we create opportunities for drama, for kinaesthetic learning through construction of posters, for example, and collaborative learning through discussion and group work. The central beliefs are clear: in order to read texts successfully, students have to have opportunities to realize Bruner's 'spiral learning' (Bruner 1966) – to critique, explore, deconstruct and reconstruct text – and to experience Eliot's 'know[ing] the place for the first time'. The centrality of involvement with others in this process is a given. With such well-established approaches to reading literary texts, the traditionalists might ask how on earth ICT can hope to contribute to, let alone enhance, reading literary texts, particularly when ICT can be seen as an isolating and linear event if interpreted to mean individual students in front of individual screens.

It is a valid point insofar as none of us involved with this chapter would want to promote use of ICT as an 'instead of established approaches'. But we are in accord in believing that ICT offers an opportunity to extend pedagogical approaches to embrace approaches which not only draw on students' (often impressive) skills in ICT use, thus placing students at the centre of learning and with clear ownership of the area (a firmly established tenet in good English teaching), but also make relevant the dominant medium of adolescent communication in the access of what the students may well see as traditional text.

What, then, are the features that our teaching colleagues consider warrant consideration of ICT in teaching literature?

Simply asking where ICT can be said to reflect and extend some of the features we refer to above, is in itself helpful. Our colleague David Greenwood identifies the following as his reasons for using ICT to teach literature. Kinaesthetic learning, for example, is for David an essential feature of ICT use in English:

> It enables the use of a much greater range of effects, the use of varying type fonts, wide use of colour, the addition of sound and imported graphics, and kinetic effects for example. The potential of such effects has been shown to have a highly motivating effect on students, especially those who are more likely to think in terms of spatial rather than verbal models.

He demonstrates too that, in his classroom, he considers group work is enhanced through the use of ICT:

ICT enables group work. It is often difficult for more than two pupils to collaborate on a conventional poster; using word processing, groups of three or more are quite possible. The talk that goes on within the group about the text and the negotiation of the text mapping outcome, develops close attention to the text itself and its recreation in visual form.

And in addressing the ways in which ICT can challenge ideas about meaning and text, David points out that:

It moves the reader from the traditional practical criticism approach where 'the words on the page' are paramount, to the more modern reader-response where the text is something to be constructed in the mind of the reader or, in the case of group work, to be negotiated among a group of readers. For further ideas on this see Rosenblatt (1938) and Fish (1980), among others. The originals can easily be downloaded from the Internet for classroom use, saving the task of typing them in and enabling more time for discussion and creation.

We turn now to consider some practical uses of ICT in secondary class-rooms and draw on two major areas of interest: thinking skills and mind mapping.

Thinking skills and mind mapping

Both thinking skills and mind mapping are familiar concepts in the English classroom. The examples which follow demonstrate how two teachers, Mary Martin and David Greenwood, have used ICT to enhance their own teaching of English through engagement with these approaches.

Thinking skills

Mary Martin, deputy head of Comberton Village College in Cambridge-shire, is well-known for her work on teaching poetry and thinking skills through ICT.

Mary writes:

Thinking skills in English are, to my mind, about constructing frame-works for thinking about text using agreed literary approaches. They are about identifying textual features, using analytical and critical language as you go, dissecting text through annotations and comment but using ICT to support that analysis in ways printed text cannot achieve.

If we take reading poetry as an example, and concern ourselves with teaching the features of poetry – voice, rhythm, rhyme, length of line, metaphor and so on – ICT enables students to identify these features in what I refer to as 'text combing': the systematic identification of features for analysis. This is easily achieved by students representing the features on screen through changing font type or size, by changing colour of text and so forth, and then examining in detail how these highlighted features allow you to understand how the poet has set out to make the poem work. If you, for example, highlight all the verb tenses and then change the tense – an easy thing to achieve with ICT – what effect does this have on the reading of the poem? Or, what is the effect of changing the gender of the narrative voice (this works very well in some of the poems in *Yesterday, Today and Tomorrow*) or changing pronouns ('How do I love him? Let me count the ways' becomes quite a different story). The effect of re-reading text in this way can be startling with respect to the insights produced, and ICT allows such activities to be undertaken quickly and easily.

Seeing text in visual form also demonstrates sound patterns effectively – alliteration and assonance, for example. This can translate into choral work through reading out loud sound patterns identified, which in turn reinforces the vitality of the language features selected by the poet.

Reading, using ICT, enables engagement with text in ways that printed text alone does not support. Asking students to manipulate text on screen gives a reason for re-reading, a skill they need to develop but which is often resisted with printed text alone.

Mind mapping

I have always thought it a pity that the world is run by literary [types] because the visual side is so much more powerful and constructive.

(Edward de Bono 1996)

David Greenwood's commitment to visual learning, illustrated by his choice of quotation above, is evident in his classroom through the use of a specific form of thinking skill: mind mapping. In the text which follows, David explores his own thinking through examples of mind mapping work from some of his students.

A divergent, creative note-making and memory-assisting, thinking skill promoting strategy which combines images and keywords, connected first to 'basic ordering ideas' and then to additional branches, 'mapping' has most often been associated with (and been undertaken with) the 'hands on' use of coloured pens and paper, as opposed to computers, until recent years. However, with the ever increasing availability of easy to use drawing programs and with the development of 'mapping' software (for example, MindManager) exponents of 'mapping', such as Tony Buzan (Buzan and Buzan 2000) and Oliver Caviglioli (Caviglioli and Harris 2000) have been promoting ICT approaches. The example below illustrates how ICT can motivate students to explore and present their reactions to texts through this exploratory, summarizing and concentration-enhancing approach: it is, in the full original version, an intelligently colourful investigation of key features of Hardy's *Far From the Madding Crowd*, from a 'big picture' perspective. The student concerned, very much enjoyed linking apposite quotations from the text with the characters' names and other literary terms – all with simple but eye-catching graphics. It was then presented to the whole class via the interactive whiteboard.

Caviglioli and Harris (2000), building on Hyerle (1996) and Buzan and Buzan (2000), states that the theory of constructivism is 'fatally ineffective without any knowledge tools to give to students to use' (p. 71). Caviglioli goes on to argue that Visual Tools, such as 'model' (or 'mind') 'maps', 'matrices' and 'double-bubble maps' can liberate short-term memory, allowing the reader and writer to organize his/her thoughts. These kinds of Visual Tools can transform thinking that is normally invisible and fleeting, into thinking that is visible and can be shared. Caviglioli feels strongly that schools need more tools now, if thinking skills are to be deployed well. For me, Caviglioli and Hyerle have done most, generically at least, to suggest practical tools for visual learners, following Howard Gardner's definitions (Gardner 1993).

Educationalists committed to constructivist ideals and practises, such as David Jonassen, believe strongly that computers can be used to support significant learning. With his 'mindtools' concept, Jonassen insists that well-chosen ICT programs and applications can, in the right hands, become 'cognitive tools . . . for engaging and enhancing multiple forms of thinking in learners' (Jonassen 2000: 3). He defines computer-based 'mindtools' as tools that have been adapted to 'function as intellectual partners with the learner' (Jonassen: 9), before listing 'critical thinking', 'creative thinking' and 'complex thinking' as being the thinking skills that can potentially be best engaged and supported (Jonassen: 27–31). I have found Jonassen's challenge to promote 'learning with computers' (Jonassen: 8) extremely helpful as I, with colleagues, have designed and used the 'mindtool' strategies here – all of these strategies have successfully brought about enhanced 'connecting', 'analyzing' and 'evaluating'. The example (Figure 3.1) based on Tennyson's *Idylls of the King*, sees a student explore the Examination criteria-related areas of study for this narrative poem (themes, characterization, poetic technique and setting) to very good effect. This student's presentation also served as a learning tool, enabling him to organize a later analysis of the poem. His sparse but strategic deployments of keywords, icons and quotations all fall within one landscape page, part of which is reproduced here.

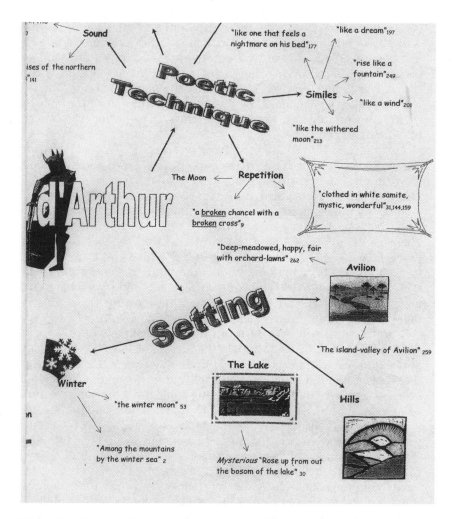

Figure 3.1 A student's presentation of Examination criteria-related areas of study for Tennyson's *Idylls of the King*

The work of both David Greenwood and Mary Martin demonstrates how ICT can enhance current teaching and learning strategies when using texts familiar to all English classrooms. This use of ICT as an approach to reading classroom texts is an important development. But ICT has impacted on reading beyond the printed text. We want now to turn to consider the ways in which texts themselves have changed – and the concomitant changes in understanding reading.

Electronic text: web pages and beyond

Our second contention, that both the reading of electronic texts and the ways in which, and the extent of the text form (for example, the place of graphics and the physical representation of text beyond the linear) make different demands on the reader. This is now a debated issue in English teaching. But the teaching of reading in this context takes, often, a lower place in the hierarchy of subject demands, if it appears at all. It is usually early in Key Stage 3 (KS3: 11–14-year-old students) to avoid the, in our view, sadly low-level demands of end of key stage tests, known widely as SATs. Key Stage 4 (KS4: 14–16-year-old students) is consumed by the need to meet GCSE demands; again, in our view, low-level but crammed with texts, as if amount is more significant than engaging with the meta-concepts involved in critiquing text. The timing of this exploration of reading electronic text is often in itself limiting. Years 7 and 8 (11–13-year-olds) are exciting years to teach in first developing an understanding of how texts work, but the sophistication of thinking about textual construction is rarely present in the ways that are needed in considering, for example, postmodernist constructions. This means that exploration of reading and form often do not recur until, and if, students encounter the concepts at A level. There are of course, always exceptions to this 'rule', but nevertheless, our contention is that this fundamental reading skill is rarely taught in the ways it might best be through the use of conventional text. Instead, the use of ICT is here an exceptional resource.

Reading web pages constitutes a substantial amount of adolescent reading activity (Lankshear and Knobel 2003). The briefest of engagement with websites reveals minimal text and maximal graphics, including animation. Indeed, 'good' websites are deemed so because of their avoidance of being 'text heavy'. Reading image is a skill taught during media, whether as a separate subject or integral to the English curriculum – and yet skills taught in one curriculum area are rarely transferred by students into another area. So the reading of web pages is rarely subject to the scrutiny of a framed shot.

Production and 'trustworthiness' (to borrow House's (1991) term in relation to validity and action research) of text are also lively concerns for website readers. Conditioned to accept the printed word (in whichever medium) as 'true', students do not spontaneously question claims made on the Internet. In fact they report using the Internet to 'check up on' other written sources in order to establish 'what is true' and will defer to the Internet site as more likely to be correct when texts contradict one another (Brindley forthcoming). Teaching about bias and provenance of text, suffers the same blind spot as other 'transferable skills'. The research quoted here also demonstrated that the ICT co-ordinators were confident that students were taught the need to filter text, through concerns about bias and provenance, and that they took this into consideration when using Internet information. The reality found by those involved in the research study (of 10 schools and nearly 100 students), was that very few students considered either of these notions when using the Internet to 'research' work. We put 'research' in inverted commas because in itself this activity is contentious: when claiming to research using the Internet, many students depressingly meant cutting and pasting information. One student claimed he had 'not read' his own course work on *Romeo and Juliet* but had simply pasted together what seemed to be relevant text – a disappointing reaction.

Form and text are an ongoing discussion for the English classroom. Excellent established practises have been in evidence for a long time. Herbert's 'Easter Wings' is a prime example of a crafted and instantly striking relationship of text and form. ICT allows a simple but powerful analysis of form and meaning through the straightforward reorganization of text into conventional stanza form. This activity reveals the power of text, shaped physically, to challenge or confirm a reading. Students can then reverse the process and literally shape text which had been created using conventional representation. (Donne and Dickinson provide rich resources for this type of activity.) Animating the text (try with Donne's 'The Flea') is even more effective in taking form and meaning a step further. On a practical (if limited level) ICT can be said to be helpful here too, in that text is readily available on the Internet and students can be asked to download and then reversion text on screen. It is quite possible to undertake some of these activities using paper resources but the preparation would be substantial and the outcome less satisfying. The gain made in these types of uses of ICT is usually time, and while this is no small event in a crowded curriculum, the learning that takes place using ICT can be said to be fundamentally different from that using paper-based resources. Text, shape and meaning are visually and immediately fundamentally interlinked. Helpful examples of this type of text can be found in Abbs and Richardson (1990).

However, ICT challenges the idea of reading form beyond the elegance and beauty of 'Easter Wings'. Where we might extend understanding of reading and form is in the use of hypertext. This commonly experienced construction of text asks students to experience text as potentially infinite, ironically without fixed form yet with complex construction. The types of texts encountered through hypertext will in themselves be many and varied in form, some with text, some with graphics, some animated, some with sound, some trustworthy and some not. Reading hypertext relies on an understanding of form and meaning which makes new reading demands. Both Ilana Snyder and Teresa Dobson expand this theme in Chapters 5 and 6.

Producing web pages is an increasingly common activity in the classroom. At A level, a recent example looking at John Fowles' *The French Lieutenant's Woman* and Jane Austen's *Persuasion* included students being allocated into research groups, with each group being allocated a particular focus (Lyme Regis/class/place of women and so forth) and being expected to edit these into a coherent set of linked pages. What is different here from the conventional 'poster and presentation' approach is that the resulting website included audio commentary, video clips, a filmed role play of a sequence from *The French Lieutenant's Woman*, links to wider reading, and an annotated set of text extracts from the two books demonstrating differences and similarities in presentation of key issues. The resulting website was then saved onto the English Faculty website and all students had free access on a permanent basis to the ideas contained there. All this sounds like fun (a much underrated quality in classrooms), and indeed it was. But the learning that was involved took these students into a dramatically enhanced understanding of 'reading the text'. The two major texts unfolded and revealed themselves as linked, not just to one another but also to an almost infinite number of other texts. In order to be effective in producing a coherent account, students had to enter the activity with a concept of reading which included not just of words, but also of graphics, audio, video and appropriate additional resources as part of the reading experience.

In this version of reading, the text is extended and branches in a limitless way, linear narrative form is no longer the dominant reading model and indeed the text can be read and re-read in quite different referential formats, depending on the routes chosen by the reader. Not only the content but also the relationship of reading one text with another can create new and unpredictable meanings.

Provisionality

Such considerations take us somewhat neatly into the realm of text and provisionality. It can be said that conventional text carries within it the expectation of closure. We read a book until we reach the end. We read reports to extract information but we expect this to be finite. Newspapers, poems, reports, TV listings, recipes, *Middlemarch* all end – and the text is fixed. We do not expect on re-reading to find the text has changed. If Macbeth is not killed by Macduff, we believe we have encountered a postmodernist version (with varying degrees of enthusiasm about that experience); if Larkin does not tell us 'Well, we shall find out', we would question whether the text had been printed correctly. But text on the Internet is neither finite nor fixed. Indeed, the whole point of ICT text locates itself within malleability. The reading model which follows from this has to be equally flexible.

In many ways, the notion of provisionality in reading has been evident in English for some time. English teachers are familiar with the idea that meaning in text is not fixed. Reader-response theory and post-structuralist approaches to text both demonstrate such a position. An example of repositioning reading and meaning can be found in the excellent *From Picture Book to Literary Theory* (Watson and Stevens 1994). The picture book *John Brown, Rose and the Midnight Cat* (Wagner 1985) is used to explore reader-response theory, that is, the theory that meaning changes in text as the reader brings differing experiences to the interpretation of that text. In this beautiful book, an elderly lady (Rose) lives with her sheepdog (John Brown) and they are clearly happy together. One night a black cat appears in the garden. Rose wants to let him into the house. John Brown resists strenuously and draws a line around the house to show the cat he is not wanted. But Rose falls ill and John Brown decides that the cat might have to be let in if Rose is to get better. The book ends with a picture of the midnight cat on the arm of Rose's chair. The question is: What is the story about? You will have your own interpretations, and all, according to reader response theory, are valid. The whole point is that narrative reflects back to you your own world views, and as these change, so might your reading of the text. Tried with a Year 7 class (11-year-olds), the most common interpretation was that John Brown was jealous. Asked for examples of jealousy from their lives, they volunteered experiences with brothers and sisters or friends. In an A level group, the observations were darker: the midnight cat represented peer jealousy, certainly, but also death. The 'magic line' John Brown draws does not keep death out; it simply delays its entrance to Rose's house and what is worse, eventually, at Rose's bidding, John Brown has to invite death in. Two different interpretations. But can it be said that either of these sets of interpretations is wrong? In being different but both convincing, they demonstrate the layering of textual meaning – and that therefore no text has a single, fixed meaning.

From the same volume by Watson and Stevens (1994) comes the post-structuralist exercise of reading *Black and White* (Macauley 1991), a large picture book with each page divided into four. Each section has a different narrative being told so that four stories unfold throughout the book. But simultaneously, the stories begin to bleed into each other. The back and white of newsprint falls into the field of the black and white cows in the picture underneath; the black and white clothing of the people in the railway station merges with the black and white of buildings. So which text do we allocate meaning to? or are there as many meanings as texts we can create from the pictures? And where does the text 'end'?

Exploration of the construction of meaning is a process which has many echoes in the notion of provisionality in text. ICT develops this post-structuralist construction of text even further. Although, as with *Black and White*, it is still possible to read text in an ICT environment as linear narrative, the activity inevitably becomes limited and less interesting. Where text changes, so does meaning. Reading ICT challenges the solidness of printed text with the seductive offer of glimpses into other worlds.

In setting aside of the notion of fixedness, the text offers up new riches of possibility. In the same ways, text constructed through ICT invites reversioning, reading beyond the linear, and the idea that the unpredictability of text makes it almost live.

The activity of reading is thus fundamentally redefined to accommodate the idea that the reader defines 'the end'; and it is the reader who will define willingness to tolerate, or enthusiasm to embrace, text that changes – provisionality. In writing, provisionality is bound up with drafting and changing text. We are more familiar with this idea in this language mode. But in reading, encountering the dancing text is unexpected. Reading becomes less an activity of accumulation, sorting and analysis of ideas in a contained and bounded environment, and more an immediate editing activity of relevance, trustworthiness and value to the original concepts being pursued. The construction of text takes on a different meaning. Most frequently associated with writing, ICT now demands that readers actively and independently 'construct' their reading text and, what is more, do so within the act of reading, not as a later event, nor indeed, given the infinity of hypertext, by planning ahead. A recent example is that of blogs and wikipedias, and the essence of both is that text changes; revisiting an entry will be an experience of updating and expanding knowledge, by contributing text, changing existing text or simply by re-reading expanded text.

Perhaps most fundamentally, though, working with provisionality of text allows us to understand the processes of construction of text: that no text remains unaltered in its production, that author re-reading (editing) is an integral part of writing, and that no text is written without being read and re-read by its author(s). This is the deep drafting. Editing the surface features of any text is addressed in the final polishing, but the ideas, the generation of thought, are the essence of any text and the provisionality of re-reading and rewriting is the evidence of this process. For the English classroom, the concept of provisionality is central in transforming drafting (for this is what provisionality is in this context) from merely the task of correcting spelling, or syntax, or grammar, into seeing these as the final stage in the longer and much more significant stages of creativity and thinking. Using the British Library website (http://www.bl.uk/onlinegallery/themes/englishlit) it is possible to download original drafted versions of poems and prose showing clearly the re-reading and drafting processes which authors go through. It is often a surprise to students to realize that text does not come fully formed, even to the most successful of writers.

Understanding that text is crafted and that all writers are readers of their own work and will produce several versions of that work, makes the realization that they too are 'real writers', and that re-reading and drafting are not a signal of failure, a revelation to many students. Entering into the writers' guild via the recognition of provisionality is a gift which ICT can bestow. Drafting is of course much less arduous using ICT. This is one advantage. It is useful to ask students to track changes so that they are able to see the successive stages through which their own writing has progressed and to compare those with the drafts from writers, who were masters at their craft. The act of re-reading drafts of one's own work is often a learning activity in itself.

Once the concept of provisionality is established, activities such as pre-quels and plot/character/genre change have greater meaning. Knowing that the text will already have been subject to major change adds a reality factor to the classroom event.

Conclusion

We began by considering the notion of e-learning as enhancement. In considering how ICT can extend existing classroom strategies in English, we have gone some way in exploring how ICT can indeed develop and augment teaching and learning in English. But we hope that we have also been able to demonstrate that the existence of ICT makes new demands on reading through e-text and how, in turn and through provisionality, those new demands lead to a more profound understanding of how text works.

We hope, too, that we have been successful to some degree in demonstrating that the concept of reading with ICT includes graphics, audio and video and that reading demands extend far beyond text. Indeed, with ICT perhaps we can change Hamlet's weary comment:

Polonius: What do you read, my lord?

Hamlet: Words, words, words.

Note

1. We are particularly indebted to Dr David Greenwood (King Edward Grammar School for Boys, Chelmsford) both for case study materials and for his section in this chapter on mind mapping. Our thanks go too to Mary Martin, Comberton Village College, Cambridge, for her contributions on thinking skills.

References

Abbs, P. and Richardson, J. (1990) *Forms of Poetry: A Practical Guide for English.* Cambridge: Cambridge University Press.

Brindley, S. (forthcoming) Secondary students' use of the Internet in learning: student perspectives on classrooms in the UK.

Bruner, J. (1966) *Toward a Theory of Instruction*. Cambridge, MA: Harvard University Press.

Buzan, A. and Buzan, B. (2000) *The Mind Map Book*. London: BBC Publications.

Caviglioli, O. and Harris, I. (2000) *Mapwise: Accelerated Learning through Visible Thinking*. London: Network Educational Press.

Cox, B. (1991) *Cox on Cox: An English Curriculum for the 1990s*. London: Hodder and Stoughton.

De Bono, E. (1996) *Teach Yourself to Think*. Harmondsworth: Penguin.

DfEE (2001) *Key Stage 3 National Strategy Framework for Teaching English: Years 7, 8 and 9*.

Fish, S. (1980) *Is There a Text in This Class? The Authority of Interpretive Communities*. Cambridge, MA: Harvard University Press.

Gardner, H. (1993) *Human Intelligence: Multiple Intelligences: The Theory in Practice*. New York, NY: Basic Books.

House, E.R. (1991) Realism in research, *Educational Researcher*, 20: 2–9, 30, 32, 106.

Hyerle, D. (1996) *Visual Tools for Constructing Knowledge*. Alexandria, VA: ASCD.

Jonassen, D. (2000) *Computers as Mindtools for Schools: Engaging Critical Thinking*. Englewood Cliffs, NJ: Prentice Hall.

Lankshear, C. and Knobel, M. (2003) *New Literacies*. Maidenhead: Open University Press.

Macauley, D. (1991) *Black and White*. New York, NY: Houghton Mifflin.

Rosenblatt, L.M. (1938) *Literature as Exploration*. New York, NY: Appleton-Century.

Wagner, J. (1985) *John Brown, Rose and the Midnight Cat*. London: Puffin.

Watson, K. and Stevens, J. (1994) *From Picture Book to Literary Theory*. Sydney: St Clair Press.

4

WHAT CAN TECHNOLOGY DO FOR/TO ENGLISH?

Chris Davies

For the most part, our reasons for using computers in schools tend to be based more on optimism than on experience, on some sense that so much capacity and potential must be capable of delivering more than we know about. As far as English teaching is concerned, certainly, there is no body of hard evidence that tells us with any precision when we should best use technology, or avoid it. Neither have we managed, in the absence of such evidence, to construct any kind of systematic theory that relates the capabilities of technology to the needs of English. Simply asserting that there are *lots* of purposes computers can serve in English does not really help.

All of us involved with English are prepared to articulate core concerns of the subject that are worth fighting to achieve and preserve, and in respect of these fundamentals it would seem reasonable to suggest that technology must either put up or shut up. What really matters in English? In what respects might technology improve how these things are achieved? It is up to those who care and know about the subject itself to work out the answers to these questions, rather than those trying to sell computers or e-learning or the knowledge economy to us. If we can build up a comprehensive theory of what technology can do *for* English, then we can make decisions about whether it is worth bothering with. In order to do that, we need to be very clear in the first place about what we actually do want English to do.

The core aims of English

The subject of English aims to provide a multi-layered array of skills and understandings relating to the English language. In recent years, there has been an increasing emphasis on a universal right of access to practical literacy (and oracy) skills, as a means of empowering learners in all areas of life: study, work and social intercourse. Important as this unarguably is, there is a real danger that it is displacing the subject's traditional commitment to less immediately practical uses of literacy: reading and writing for its own value, for pleasure, for altering consciousness – *deep literacy*.

This is a fundamental matter of faith for many English teachers. In the state of deep literacy, we go somewhere inside ourselves that is essential, highly charged, private; on occasions achieving the 'flow' experience described by Czikszentmihalyi and Czikszentmihalyi (1988). We use literacy in this kind of way to pass the time, cut ourselves off from the world, resolve problems or prepare ourselves for sleep. It is a very significant kind of special consciousness, as Philip Pullman vividly conveys in the following account of writing a story:

> . . . all around you is silence. And plenty of time. You're in a calm state of mind, not asleep, not at all sleepy, but calm and relaxed and attentive: not the sort of heavy stupor you fall into after several hours' television, but the sort of unharassed awareness that we achieve when we're truly absorbed. True calm intense relaxed attention.
>
> (Pullman 2003)

English teachers have long valued this aspect of their subject, despite the fact that classrooms are not at all conducive to any kind of intense inward experience because they are too busy, too noisy, too pressured and too diverse. It takes real determination to achieve experiences of deep literacy in school settings, and the UK government's Key Stage 3 Strategy, which firmly prioritizes dynamic and practical learning activities over extended reading and composition, provides little support or encouragement in that direction:

> There is clearly a balance to be achieved between providing classroom time to support the reading of longer texts, and the imperative to secure progression. Having clear objectives lends pace and focus to the study of longer texts; there is less need to teach all possible angles on the text and more reason to focus on those aspects which cluster around the objectives. The aim is to provide enjoyable encounters, which serve the

objectives well but do not demand a disproportionate commitment of time. Teachers already use a repertoire of techniques (such as the use of priority passages, support tapes, abridgement, televised extracts and recapitulation) to move quickly through longer texts without denying attention to the details and quality of the text.

(DfEE 2001: 15)

That is the reality of most classrooms now, across the curriculum: focused on achievement, full of pace, drawing on a wide range of resources, strategies, devices and games to make learning possible in the unfavourable setting of classrooms, in determinedly businesslike and focused ways. And the more that is the case, the more relevant digital technologies appear to be within the subject. But if we are serious about the question whether technology really has a useful job to do for the English subject area, we must assess its contribution in relation to all key aspects of the subject, which I have, with stunning indifference to the National Curriculum, divided up into the following three core categories:

- *Literacy basics*: learning to read and write; spelling; grammar.
- *Practical literacy and oracy*: gathering, managing and evaluating information; presentation, communication and interaction; the study of English language and literature.
- *Deep literacy*: sustained intensive reading and writing.

Given that the focus here is on English at the secondary level, I will steer clear of the very specialized (meaning: I know nothing about this) question of whether technology helps the learning of literacy basics. In the remainder of this chapter, therefore, I will concentrate on what digital technologies might do for practical literacy/oracy, and then for deep literacy.

Practical literacy and oracy

This section looks at three different cases of using technology in English that all relate to the practical and applied aspect of the subject.

Presentation, communication and interaction

At the heart of the practical application of literacy and oracy is *dialogue*, by which I mean, very broadly, communication with others. The key elements of dialogue are the capacity to express yourself, to listen to others, and to play your part in the social construction of meaning by weighing your own words and thoughts against those of others. Dialogue entails awareness of language, of the ways in which one person's ways of using words will ebb and flow in relation to another's, and awareness that understandings can be stimulated, reshaped and sometimes negated by another's. Dialogue is about taking your place in the world: learning to make yourself heard, learning to listen.

Whereas dialogue was until very recently viewed as spoken conversation between two or more people, together in the same space or perhaps at either end of a telephone line, we are now all quite familiar with the extension of possibilities for dialogue via constantly increasing numbers of media. In the normal world of young people, digital technologies have turned digitally mediated dialogue into a way of life. The considerable apparent disadvantages of dialogue, unsupported by eye contact (such as mobile phone conversations) or merely through the digitized written word (email, texting, chatrooms, bulletin boards) in no way manage to make electronic dialogue less enticing than face to face conversation; quite the contrary. Of course, for young people the vast preponderance of such dialogue is not a technical challenge: they do not need to be taught how to use it, any more than they need to be taught what to say. But they do need to be taught to explore its potential, how to apply it to a wider range of life needs, and how to grow through it.

This, out of all the ways in which technology can be really useful in achieving the most valued aspects of English, must be a leading prospect for its contribution to this particular subject – a point that has been made many times in the ICT literature, but one which has not yet become widely manifest in normal practice. The most impressive evidence for this potential that we encountered in our own recent classroom-based research investigations was in fact in a religions education lesson where, not surprisingly, specifically linguistic perspectives were not picked up by the teacher.

This lesson involved a project that lasted for about four lessons, over a period of three to four weeks. A local religious education teacher had, through a sequence of pure serendipity, set up an email communication with a school in the state of Kentucky. The project aimed to help a British Year 10 class and its American equivalent to explore ethical/religious issues relating to capital punishment, with the climax of the project consisting of a dialogue between individuals from the two classes on either sides of the Atlantic. The English and American teachers respectively presented information to their own and each other's classes about the laws, practices and beliefs relating to capital punishment in their own countries before raising some key questions as the basis for an email debate between students.

The project worked well, due in large part to the time spent building up understandings and opinions during its initial stages so that, when the time came for the students to discuss and argue through their own positions, there was already an ensured common ground between them. The energy and confidence with which the students eventually engaged in some quite tough discussion about very different views on the topic of capital punishment (expressing a fairly firm and clear-cut difference between countries regarding the topic, the English students being considerably more liberal than their American counterparts) was impressive, and could not have been achieved without the technology. It was not simply the fact that this avoided the almost insurmountable problem of time lag that would have occurred if letters had been posted – the extremely familiar and easy medium of email enabled rapid and surprisingly confident composition of responses that both argued cogent cases from each side of the discussion, and stimulated experiments with unfamiliar uses of language that both respected the discourse of the other side of the discussion, and challenged it at the same time. The following two extracts from what the UK students wrote in reply to some slightly overblown American statements give some flavour of the exchanges that took place:

Example 1
If you remember back to the Abortion debate the Americans were very vocal that it should never be allowed, even when the mother could die, based on their strong religious beliefs – thou shalt not kill etc. However now that the subject is capital punishment only an average of 30% of you base their beliefs on their religion. Furthermore more Americans are in favour of the death penalty that the British, who are supposedly less moral and religious. Do you not see this as hypocritical when you consider that Jesus was very explicit in the need for reform rather than revenge? How do you justify your strong support for capital punishment, which is in itself a very costly process and against the fundamentals of Christianity? Look forward to your response,

Example 2
we too over here tink dat capital Punishment is really very truly deeply morally wrong. for your clarification we (nic and Steve) feel it is ALWAYS wrong in ANY case. jus cos were like that. do not stereotype the whole british student body on our opinions. Capital puinishment is WACK!
  peace

The power of this activity to stimulate thoughtful experiments with discourse was highlighted towards the end of the final lesson when some students, having completed their dialogue across the Atlantic in a style created to make an impact on their American counterparts, then went on to email friends locally in order to tell them about what they had just been doing. In these emails (which were not produced as part of the official lesson, and therefore were not possible to collect as examples) the students slipped into a very different discourse, both self-mocking and super-informal. Of course, that does also suggest that some students moved through this activity with such notable energy and application because it incidentally enabled them to spend a few unexpected minutes of school time engaged in the unofficial activity of emailing friends, and that should not be mistaken for an inherently educational aspect of using ICT in school. But the fact that these students were able to switch codes with such élan in their uses of email does suggest that there is a kind of natural harmony for this aspect of English learning between content and technology.

Being a religions education lesson, though, the opportunity was not taken to build on the linguistic aspects of what had been achieved: the teacher's intention was quite clearly to give her students a stimulating experience of thinking through an ethical/spiritual issue, and this she achieved superbly. But it is exciting to imagine what an English teacher's characteristic preoccupation with language might have been able to make of the linguistic dimension that did emerge: helping the students to move to an analysis of the discourses they found themselves using with such surprising ease and fluidity; exploring how they were able to switch their dialogue between shared and complicit discourse with friends, and something more formal and postured with those with whom they were in structured dialogic contention.

The introduction of broadband into all UK classrooms should mark a moment when such experiments with dialogue and – in English lessons specifically – the analysis of the outcomes of these, in the context of real-time, meaningful engagements with others, become a central activity within the subject. Our own observations of the impact of broadband Internet access in one local education authority showed remarkably little of this taking place, which is why I had to choose an example from religions education, but that in itself is no bad thing, in that it illustrates one key aspect of a successful venture of this kind: the setting up of a genuine debate about issues that do have some meaning and involvement for the participants.

Accessing, managing and evaluating knowledge and information

Information gathering is currently the main way that teachers, in most subjects across the curriculum, make use of classroom broadband connectivity. The ease and speed of access, the almost limitless variety of material available, and the motivational benefits ought, in theory, to be stunning. Most of the teachers we spoke to in our own study of the ways teachers use broadband in the classroom felt that for the first time they could begin to take the availability and accessibility of Internet material for granted, without having to worry about the management problems that result from young people sitting in front of sluggishly responding machines, steadily losing all interest or involvement in the intended activity.

But not every teacher sees it that way. 'The problem of children "web wandering" – using the faster access to download and play games, explore websites which are unrelated to the classroom objective – is an important theme of classroom management attributed by the teachers to the speed of broadband access' (Becta 2003). What appears at first to be a simple management problem, in which the attractions of independent learning opportunities suddenly reveal themselves to have encouraged rather more independence than was actually intended, is shown to be a far more substantial issue relating to broadband's ease of access: the planning of classroom activities using any kind of Internet connection demands new and uncharted routines and skills on the part of the teacher. Apart from the more acute occasional dangers of accessing harmful material, the problem of avoiding a high-tech engagement with trivial or peripheral material is real and ever present, and the reduction in quality of learning is all the more worrying because it can be obscured by the dazzle of technology. Sometimes you do have to ask whether a particular use of Google was *really* worth the effort: 'In another food technology lesson, the students were researching pizza toppings using search engines' (Becta 2003).

This is something we encountered in a number of lessons, including English. There seemed to be a number of different individual reasons behind the fact that teachers were putting up with substandard material on occasions but these, if sufficiently frequent, are bound to lead to a worrying cumulative effect for students across the curriculum. Teachers were frequently accessing material that was new to them, working constantly with technological limitations (poor school networks, old hardware) that countered the advantages of broadband. Whether via Google or an educational website, the quality of material found on the Internet is far more random and variable than is normally considered acceptable in a formal educational setting. Even material of variable quality need not be a problem if the students are orientated towards what they find in sufficiently structured and critical ways. This, however, requires a considerable allocation of effort and time to the job of conceptualizing the search for material in the first place, especially in terms of learning to think about the questions that are worth asking of a search engine.

Teachers have long known that the Internet is, in many respects, a kind of super-plagiarism machine, and have consequently made efforts to discourage mere copying and pasting of material. As a result, students have begun to develop impressive skills of recall and précis, evident in this exchange between two students nearing the end of a sequence of two English lessons spent paraphrasing some particularly turgid and simplistic material about life in the 1920s:

G: so now we know they only had dark blue (.) dark brown (.) and charcoal colours (*dictating*) men wore (.) men *only* wore dark blue (.) dark brown and charcoal colours

B: (*finishes typing*) what was the clothes called (.) flannel (.) flannel something

G: (*reading text*) man in a grey flannel suit (*maximizes Word document and dictates*) and grey flannel suits
    (*G and B argue for two minutes over the spelling of 'gray'*)
G: now we need to do women
    (*pretty soon here, the effort to paraphrase fades*)
G: (*reading text*) Women dressed 'smartly' in the Twenties. Good grooming and a tailored look were prized. Acting and looking 'every inch the lady' –
B: so women dressed smartly –
G: just copy that (.) copy it (.) copy it all (*laughing*)
B: (*copies and pastes and reformats text*) yeah that'll do

The real and profound problem here is that the material used was simply not good enough: it had been used because it was easy to find and because it sort of related to the topic, although it revealed practically nothing of real relevance to it – a fact that is patently evident from its marked failure to stimulate the students' interest. Given such weak material, it was very difficult to find ways of getting the students to interrogate what they (guided by the teacher, through his preparatory work) encountered on the Internet. 'That'll do' is a common mantra when it comes to using Google.

Because it was self-evidently poor material, the teacher found himself forced to assert that, 'It's a very difficult skill making notes off the Internet. It's not easy. It's vital. It's a life skill', as if the irrelevance of the material studied to the English-subject focus could at least be justified because the students were at least being prepared for the broader business of using the Internet in their lives generally. All the same, the teacher was also understandably satisfied with the facts that (1) a very difficult class had been consistently on task for two whole lessons, (2) the technology had hardly gone wrong once and, (3) one more piece of course material was in the bag.

So what is the role of this kind of activity in English? While not a primarily information-focused subject, there are many specific reasons for accessing reference and background material in the study of historical contexts of literature, or the development of language and communications, and even more reasons for learning to evaluate and critique such material. To the extent that it merely resources the study of specific content, there is nothing unique about how the subject of English makes use of technology. It is, as with all subjects, a matter of developing skills in asking truly useful questions of a search engine, which we saw done superbly by A level history students who spent several weeks working out the most appropriate keywords for a particular topic through a process of prior reading and analysis, before actually going to the Internet and looking for answers. This takes time and, as James Gleick (2000) showed in *Faster*, we tend to favour speed as one of the chief benefits of technology. We need to slow down.

I am not suggesting that we restrict our information searches and explorations of contextual background in English studies to the printed word in libraries. There is some amazing stuff out there on the Internet that can be found nowhere else. But I do think the skills of looking for appropriate and illuminating material, assessing it, and then knowing how to use it properly, take a very long time to acquire, both for teachers and students. Teachers need far more time than is normally allowed by their working lives, in order to search the Internet for the kinds of things they want their students to find: the Internet is definitely *not* a timesaver in this respect.

Teachers have also got to spend considerable time working *with* their students in this process, as a collaborative enterprise in which the more expert support the less expert, whoever is whichever. The fact is that, skilful as some young people are at finding and assessing Internet material, the quality of learning can only really be monitored by teachers and, now that high-speed Internet access is available, I think that we face a genuine and serious threat to that quality because there is a lot of inaccurate (or worse) material out there. And I certainly do not think that educational websites are the solution here, for the simple reason that the criteria guiding any seriously worthwhile search ought to be too specific and demanding to be satisfied by the soggy material thrown up by broad category searches.

I think that the jury is still out on this aspect of technology's contribution to English. It all depends, in the end, on what you want to achieve by bringing English into contact with technology in the first place. This is an issue that I will come back to at the end of this chapter.

Literature study

I have included literature study under 'practical literacy and oracy' rather than under 'deep literacy' as this kind of study is one of the practical jobs that practical literacy must fulfil for learners. For instance, the study of Shakespeare at Key Stage 3 does not generally constitute an experience of deep literacy for most students, even if on occasions it might come somewhere near it. For the most part, such study is about learning to perform certain acts of literacy (such as writing specific kinds of answers to examination questions about a scene from Shakespeare) for certain institutional purposes that for the most part do not include or require a deep and intensive experience of reading or writing. It is a job to be done and teachers quite reasonably look for whatever tool will help them through it most effectively, including technology. Technology, after all, does jobs for us.

A software product that does this particular job very effectively is Immersive Education's *kar2ouche*, the use of which I and my colleagues researched in some detail during its developmental stages. *kar2ouche* is a storyboard program which enables students to select combinations of images relating to *Macbeth* from a range of alternatives stored in a databank. These take the form of illustrated backgrounds, characters and props. Students can choose a setting they consider appropriate, where in that setting to place a character (in the foreground or background, centre-stage, to the left or right), in which direction he or she should face (towards or away from the audience or another character), and the posture he or she should adopt (to suggest anger, worry, resignation, determination and so forth).

Students can then attach speech and thought bubbles to the characters and insert into them any text they choose to type, including extracts from the play itself. They are also free to type any notes they wish into a caption box which accompanies each frame. The program allows students to save the frames they render in this fashion and to display each frame in succession to suggest movement and flow from one element of a scene to the next. The program was presented in terms of helping the children to think of themselves as directors of the play, but actually it did something both more straightforward and more profound: it helped the students to discover and express their own thoughts and understandings about the play, by allowing them to create and manipulate visualizations of scenes on their own terms, as this typical kind of comment from a Year 9 student demonstrates:

> We chose that castle because it looks all eerie and kind of creepy and mysterious. He's got his hand on his head because he's feeling, when he says in his soliloquy, upset and he's decided he doesn't want to kill Duncan.

The evidence we collected from this first stage of the research (Birmingham and Davies 2002) clearly showed students using interpretation in interesting ways in order to link the text to their visualizations. When making sense of a specific scene, the students would sometimes start by creating an image on screen or talking about lines of text. In each case, in order to move back and forth between text and visualization, they would create their own explanations of what was going on in the text, as illustrated by the image they were creating on screen. In effect, what we observed was something ICTs could uniquely provide: a powerful means of visualizing ideas about the text that actually seemed to improve the quality of thinking about the words. This was far more than playing with computers as a way of diverting attention away from the realities of studying Shakespeare.

Our second stage of research involved the extensive study of two Year 9 classes using *kar2ouche* as part of their preparation for the Key Stage 3 English SATs. As it turned out – and consistent with our previous experience – the program went down very well, and both teacher and students persisted in wanting to use it over far more lessons than we had anticipated. As a result of this experience, we were able to identify three broad benefits which together constitute a good case in support of teachers' making the painful effort to incorporate ICTs into their classroom work:

1. Cognitive gain

The visualization processes of the software had a dramatic effect on the capacity of many children to think independently about the meaning of difficult text, and to make their own imaginative but usually legitimate (because based closely on specific textual examples) interpretations of that text. Our longer-term study both confirmed and extended the experience of the first stage in this respect: the process of visualization did seem to stimulate and structure quite complex thinking about texts, as the following comments from three different students indicate:

> . . . you can choose poses. You can open your imagination and you can think how you think they're going to look when they say the words. It helps you understand more.

> I just like making my own version of *Macbeth*. You can show other people. When you're writing in a book or drawing pictures it will take a long time. This is a lot quicker. It's good.

> You read the text and it's about how it sounds to you, how you read it. You put the characters acting as if how you picture them to be.

2. Motivational gain

In any use of technology, it is important to question whether enthusiasm can be maintained once novelty had worn off. The extended use of the software over several weeks – especially in the context of its being incorporated into the teachers' ongoing and pressured SATs-related priorities – did appear to sustain enthusiasm and motivation. One of the teachers explained to us that she particularly valued the impression the students had of playing a game while maintaining a good level of appropriate thinking about what was going on in the play. This experience of the software did seem to support what is often claimed on behalf of ICTs: that they can be more fun than ordinary learning.

> If you've got a textbook you tend to mess about because there's nothing else to do.

> I usually natter a lot in lessons, but in lessons using *kar2ouche* I'm just silent because I can't wait to get on with the next scene.

3. Interactional gain

The most powerful aspect of the software lies in its potential for bringing about a shift in the working relations between students and teachers. We observed many varying instances of how the on-screen work became the focus for non-confrontational negotiations between teacher and students about the tasks to be done. Not only did these negotiations reveal students' understandings of tasks as set by their teacher, in terms of the order of their constituent activities, but they also revealed students' interpretations of the pace at which they ought to proceed with tasks and their justifications for creatively deviating from them. At the same time, it appeared that students felt more ownership of the work and, more confident in their ability to explain their developing ideas to the teacher, directing the teacher's attention to particular things they had done on screen, and actually leading the way in such conversations.

> . . . it puts your imagination in the spotlight. It makes other people understand how you're thinking of it, how I'm relating to it, how I think these characters are acting, and all that. Those things get recognized.

Some students felt very positive about how such work helped them to work cooperatively, even if not all were quite as starry-eyed as the following extract suggests:

> . . . we'll both read through it together and depending on how the other characters are placed and where it is then we'll decide who's right and wrong . . . When you're working in pairs on the computer you can both put down your ideas and it makes it more interesting. We'll talk about it, and I'll say 'well I think that looks good', and if she says she'd rather do something else she would do the next scene. But we do try to get half and half in the work.

When the software was first being developed, one teacher told us that he thought it looked like glorified Fuzzy Felt, the implication of which was that this was simply an expensive way of doing what could be done just as well in more traditional ways. But I don't think he was right. The evidence of our research into this software, suggests that its benefits resulted from specifically *digital* aspects of its functionality: speed, responsiveness, memory, visual quality and (because it is used on a screen that can be viewed by several people at once) accessibility and shareability. All of these played their part in achieving each of the three kinds of benefit: cognitive, motivational and interactive. *kar2ouche* is certainly not the only computer program capable of creating these effects (even a presentational program such as PowerPoint could offer some equivalent kinds of functionality), but I certainly do not think that such effects could be achieved in the same way at this level *without* digital resources.

This experience clearly provides some degree of evidence that core aspects of English learning can be better achieved with the help of technology. It is true that generalized benefits of enthusiasm and classroom management (in particular, because the screen seems to become a constructive, non-confrontational mediating space between teacher and student) can be considered desirable in all subjects, but even with regard to these there is also an English-specific element: the importance of learners in this subject feeling confident and free to *interpret* texts in their own terms, along with an obligation to argue that interpretation with peers or with the teacher. Such desirable behaviour might not be restricted to English, but it is surely a particularly salient feature of the subject, and there were instances in our *kar2ouche* observations where the learners seemed to be going beyond the mere preparation of answers for their impending SATs:

> . . . it makes you think about what they're thinking, and if you think about what they're thinking it makes you understand what they're trying to say more.

> . . . when you're reading the books it's only your imagination you've got to use. It's like what *you're* thinking.

> . . . it puts your imagination in the spotlight. It makes other people understand how you're thinking of it, how I'm relating to it, how I think these characters are acting, and all that. Those things get recognized.

Such cognitive gain was the most specifically English element: the capacity of this program to encourage the development of half-formulated internal thoughts into a line of argument capable of being expressed to an external audience, offered more than simply getting-the-job-done functionality. We encountered repeated evidence with regard to some individuals of deep engagement in texts, and of autonomous reflection on meaning, that were undeniably generated by using digital technology.

Deep literacy

The third core aspect of English – deep literacy – concerns the way in which concentration upon the written word can take you deep inside your own head. This is not really about communicating with others at all. It is the personal, interior aspect of English, and it is not an easy state to achieve whether through reading or writing. There is a lot of competition from easier activities, a great number of more immediately appealing ways to pass the time or escape the daily working world. English teachers have a very important job to do, encouraging young people to open themselves up to the possibilities and habit of deep literacy as a viable and even just occasional alternative to TV or games playing; but this is what English teachers do.

The question that concerns us here is how, if at all, computers can help in this respect. Have digital technologies something unique to offer in terms of enabling young people to find their ways into deep literacy, and for that to become an important part of their lives? In terms of their relationship to technology, writing and reading are two very different routes to the same place, and they need to be considered quite separately.

Writing

PCs process words; it is one of the main things they do, especially in offices. For those of us whose working lives are constructed around a desk with a computer on it, the computer screen and keyboard have become the main focus and medium of writing. The benefits and disadvantages of using word processors for writing, are at times quite finely balanced for even the most experienced adult writers; indeed, most of the benefits can prove to be mixed blessings. Being able to churn out good looking text at high speed, to move it around, store it away, work with multiple versions, edit, correct, recycle and delete, can land the most practised writer in deep water, to the extent that these facilities can sometimes prove to be quite paralysing. Nonetheless, and despite all these dangers, it is self-evidently the case that individuals *can* enter into deep and intense compositional states in front of the computer screen. People use computers to write things they genuinely care about, not just memos and invoices.

Young people in school do not, for the most part, experience writing on computer screens in the same way. They do not have anything like continuous access in classrooms, nor are they particularly practised in using the functionality of word processing. The disadvantages generally must outweigh any benefits, at least when it comes to settling down to sustained writing of any kind, especially creative. The computer might be brilliant for helping children and young people do all sorts of worthwhile learning jobs in the classroom, but is it realistic to expect computers to help them write at length, or in depth? That would be quite an achievement, given how difficult it is to get many young people to write at length without them.

I definitely do think this is possible, and perhaps uniquely so, for fairly good reasons and despite the immense logistical difficulties of finding the kind of concentration space in classrooms or elsewhere (in school *or* at home – see Facer *et al.* 2003) where an individual child can sit in front of a computer screen and focus on the act of writing. It is uniquely possible because the functionality of word processors is particularly helpful to those who cannot write much: computer screens are responsive, they make the writing look good, and they normalize writing in ways that are not even viewed as writing (email, chatrooms, web pages and so on). In addition, some of the (slightly more) advanced structural features of word processors, such as Word's Outline View, offer a degree of organizational oversight and control that is simply not available with the written word.

Many of these benefits have not been explored, and I suspect little ground has been covered in thinking about how to ameliorate the logistical difficulties of using computers in the classroom in order to enhance opportunities for serious, sustained written composition. I suspect that awareness of some children's poor keyboard skills figures in here also, to some extent. It might just all seem out of reach, but I think that is a mistaken view for the long term. English teachers urgently need to start experimenting with this aspect of technology in the subject.

Reading

This need not detain us for long. What works for writing has no relevance to reading, when it comes to technology. Computers might well have some part to play in supporting 'reading', the broad range of curriculum targets that come under this general category which cover the ground of reading, at a meta-level. I have already quoted the shameless encouragement from the Key Stage 3 Strategy to use lots of strategies in order to obviate the time-consuming problem of reading long texts through 'the use of priority passages, support tapes, abridgement, televized extracts and recapitulation' (DfEE 2001: 15). If it is ways of short-circuiting the difficulties of finding time and space to read in school that we are after, then I suppose that computers might prove to be as efficacious as televized extracts and support tapes.

I see no reason why we need to switch on a computer in order to read a book, except if that can in any way overcome the problems experienced in some parts of the world in getting hold of books. But if you have got books, then why not use them? They are quite the most successful technology for reading that has come along so far – the whole business of bound paper pages that you turn over and read through in a particular order still works really well. Sony and others did try to manufacture electronic books (receiving a massive raspberry of indifference for their efforts) and in fact most attempts at replicating reading on screen involve some attempt at replicating the turning paper page also, which seems to be rather missing the point. And if it was really possible to read text easily on screen, how come everyone's got to have a printer?

At a more conceptual level of reading, I recall some degree of excitement a few years back about how hypertext would transform the act of reading. Sequential linearity was out, replaced by the notion of moving through texts in random and unexpected directions, leaping from one hyperlink to the next, one text to the next, representing a challenging future for the reader as much as the writer. There is no doubt that we need to work with young learners, and with older learners for that matter, on how to manage what is in reality a disconcerting way of engaging with the world, in which serendipity becomes the route to all discovery and learning, and in which you virtually never reach the end of any single text. Postmodernist decentred texts probably have their attractions, but I suspect that they are the antithesis of any kind of deep literacy. If we just want to see more children more often sitting down and reading at length, silently, then this is a no-brainer: all you need is a book, and the opportunity to read it.

Conclusion

In this chapter I have tried to think through the ways in which we might talk about technology in English. I have argued that technology has got to prove its worth within the subject, both because it is bothersome (expensive, unreliable, disruptive), and because it has the power to lead us away from the things we care about most in English. Those things change with the times, and will continue to change as technology becomes steadily, but very slowly, more established on the educational landscape.

We must look beyond those bothersome characteristics (although these are surprisingly resilient), to the questions of what technology can do *for* English, and what it might do *to* the subject in the process. Digital technologies are too powerful to settle for simply being tools for achieving the old familiar things, and we need to be open minded and suspicious about them in equal measure.

These technologies, as I have tried to illustrate in this chapter, can provide unrivalled opportunities for exploring the communicative power of language, in brand new ways that, for instance, blur the traditional distinctions between written and spoken language. They can also be immensely powerful in helping young people to visualize, explore and express thoughtful ideas about difficult texts. They might also prove capable of expanding young people's readiness and capacity to write at length, and this is something which I believe we should explore with considerably more focus and energy.

At the same time, there are some aspects of these technologies that are, I believe, at odds with the best aims of English. As well as being an amazing worldwide network of communication and democratic self-expression, the Internet is also a bottomless source of misinformation, and of ugly shoddy material: access to the Internet can as easily reduce the quality of learning in a classroom as expand it. We have to engage with that, because the Internet is a major and insistent part of our lives. As a global medium of communication, I think that it belongs fairly and squarely within the scope of English, but it is not at all evident that we yet understand enough about how to deal with that fact. Meanwhile, the monster grows and grows, and eats up more and more time: time that might better be spent reading a book.

There are a lot of contradictions here, which I think we need to take seriously. Just because technology is uniquely able to achieve *some* important aspects of English, it certainly does not mean that it is good for *all* aspects. It is unforgivable to waste the power of technology when it can do real good, but we need suffer no qualms about leaving it in its box the rest of the time.

References

Becta (2003) Technology Intelligence Unit, unpublished report.

Birmingham, P. and Davies, C. (2002) Storyboarding Shakespeare: learners' interactions with storyboard software in the process of understanding difficult literary texts, *Journal of Information Technology for Teacher Education*, 10(3).

Czikszentmihalyi, M. and Czikszentmihalyi, I. (1988) *Optimal Experience: Psychological Studies of Flow in Consciousness*. Cambridge: Cambridge University Press.

DfEE (2001) *Key Stage 3 National Strategy Framework for Teaching English: Years 7, 8 and 9*.

Facer, K., Furlong, J., Furlong, R. and Sutherland, R. (2003) *ScreenPlay: Children and Computing in the Home*. London: RoutledgeFalmer.

Gleick, J. (2000) *Faster: The Acceleration of Just About Everything*. London: Abacus.

Pullman, P. (2003) Isis lecture, 1 April 2003. Available at http://www.philip-pullman.com/pages/content/index.asp?PageID=66.

5

NEW MEDIA AND CULTURAL FORM: NARRATIVE VERSUS DATABASE

Ilana Snyder

Why narrative and database

Stories define how we think, how we play, even how we dream: they represent a basic way of organizing human experience. We understand our lives through stories. Barbara Hardy has argued famously, that narrative is 'a primary act of mind transferred to art from life' (Hardy 1977: 12). The act of the storyteller, the author, the novelist, says Hardy, arises from what we do all the time, in remembering, dreaming and planning.

Narrative is so deeply ingrained as a cultural form that we take for granted the ways in which storytelling engages our interest, curiosity, fear, tensions, expectations and sense of order:

> For we dream in narrative, daydream in narrative, remember, anticipate, hope, despair, believe, doubt, plan, revise, criticize, construct, gossip, learn, hate, and love by narrative. In order really to live, we make up stories about ourselves and others, about the personal as well as the social; past and future.
>
> (Hardy 1977: 13)

Indeed, narrative is so familiar that it has become naturalized: we are no longer conscious of its significance for the ways in which we live our lives.

There is an important explanation for why this has come to be: the novel and cinema, with their pervasive influence, have privileged the narrative as the key form of cultural expression of the modern age. However, we are now in the computer age, which, proclaims Lev Manovich (2001), has introduced narrative's correlate: the computer database. As Manovich explains:

> Many new media objects do not tell stories; they do not have a beginning or end; in fact, they do not have any development, thematically, formally, or otherwise that would organize their elements into a sequence. Instead, they are collections of individual items, with every item possessing the same significance as any other.
>
> (Manovich 2001: 218)

What is a database? Like narrative, a database represents a basic way of organizing human experience. A database can be a library, a museum, in fact any large collection of cultural data. In the age of the Internet, a database is a structured collection of data organized to maximize fast search and retrieval by computer. It represents a potentially powerful categorization system as it provides a range of options for sorting and viewing sets of data.

Somewhat loosely, but also generatively, Manovich (2001) uses the word as a metaphor to denote how a collection of digital data can be searched, navigated and viewed in a variety of ways (Walton in press). Unlike a narrative, which creates a cause-and-effect trajectory of seemingly unordered items or events, a database appears to users as a collection of items to view, navigate and search, no matter how it is organized. As a cultural form – a general way used by the culture to represent human experience, the world and human existence in the world – the database represents life as a list of items and does not presume to order the list.

This explains why the experience of using such a collection of information is different from reading a story or watching a film. According to Manovich (2001), these two contrasting cultural forms now dominate the landscape of new media.

In this chapter, I examine how narrative and database manifest themselves, interconnect, perhaps compete, in the context of new media, most often conceived as the Internet, websites, computer multimedia, computer games, CD-ROMS and DVD, and virtual reality. The focus here, however, is on just two of these manifestations: games and websites. Although in education, and in the social sciences more broadly, the terms 'information and communication technologies' (ICTs) or simply 'new technologies' are more commonly used, I prefer 'new media' as the term accommodates a greater range of technologies. It also informs the notion of a new media revolution: the shift of culture to computer-mediated forms of production, distribution and communication.

As is often the case when a new technology or a new way of organizing and making sense of the world comes along, we have the opportunity to 'make the familiar strange': to reappraise what we think we know about our world and how we do things within it. The birth of the World Wide Web in the early 1990s, together with the extraordinary speed of its uptake and expanding influence, at least in the developed world, is one such instance. If the database form is becoming increasingly important as a way of organizing information and data, perhaps at the expense of narrative, then we need to make sure that we understand the nature of the new form, how it differs from narrative and also, importantly, how the two inter-relate. We also need to consider if indeed there has been a cultural shift of the magnitude alleged by Manovich (2001) and if so, its implications for literacy education.

Integral to my discussion, is the belief that providing opportunities for students to deepen and refine their capacity for informed and critical response to the significant cultural forms associated with the use of new media needs to be recognized as an important goal of literacy education. This outcome is more likely to be achieved if teachers understand for themselves the nature of these cultural forms in the context of the use of new media, share, even if imperfectly, the language with which to talk about them and have real opportunities to consider how best to reorganize their classrooms and their approaches to teaching and learning in creative ways when these new media are used. The questions posed in this chapter about the relationship between narrative and database are critical, as they have profound implications for the effective design of curriculum frame-works and teachers' in-service and pre-service programmes that take account of new media.

It might appear that the structure of this chapter pits narrative and database against each other, thus creating an artificial opposition, when in reality their relationship is something more complex and nuanced. How-ever, as a self-conscious rhetorical device, discussing them separately serves to highlight the differences between them, thereby providing a base upon which greater understanding of their interconnections may be built.

It might also seem that too much attention is given to defining and explaining key concepts. The concepts selected for explanation, however, are integral to understanding the cultural shifts which provide the focus of this chapter. Probably, because of their unfamiliarity, some of these words, such as 'compositing' and 'interface', may seem ugly, even alienating. Fur-ther, as Raymond Williams (1976) points out, there are difficulties in any kind of definition because the meanings of words – such as 'narrative' and 'database' – are embedded in relationships and in processes of social and historical change. No word ever finally stands on its own; it is always an element in the social process of language.

However, the words and their meanings that receive extended treatment are foundational to a potentially illuminating discussion of literacy in a world increasingly mediated by the use of new electronic technologies. Each word has somehow demanded my consideration because the problems of its meaning seem bound up with the problems I am using it to discuss. Of course, the complex issues surrounding teaching, learning and the use of new media cannot be understood simply by analysing the words used to discuss them. But, at the same time, the issues cannot really be thought through unless we are conscious of the words as elements of the problems. Thus, not only the argument central to this chapter but also the meanings of the words used to drive it are given attention.

Finally, it could be construed that I have drawn heavily on the work of just one theorist in the area of new media – Lev Manovich – perhaps ignoring other important thinkers. I hope that readers will agree with me that Manovich's (2001) book *The Language of New Media* raises a number of provocative, most likely unfamiliar, yet highly relevant ideas for literacy educators. Indeed, I have drawn on just one small element of the book when so much more could be usefully employed to inform the teaching of English in an electronic world.

Understanding narrative in the context of new media

Reconceiving narrative theory

In the context of new media, narrative manifested itself initially as electronic adventure games, then interactive fiction, followed soon after by hyperfiction. All these forms continue to exist, indeed, they are all flourishing in their present instantiations. Much has been written about the literary precursors to electronic narrative (Snyder 1996). Suffice it to say here that since the beginning of modern fiction, authors have attempted to cajole readers out of passivity. Literary precursors of interactive fiction and hyperfiction include not only *Tristram Shandy* and *Ulysses*, but also more recent fiction, such as Julio Cortazar's *Hopscotch* (1966) and Borges' *Labyrinths* (1970). All work strenuously against the medium in which their books are produced. In attacking the convention that a novel is a coherent narrative of events, such texts simultaneously invite and confirm reader interaction.

Because interactive fiction already existed in print and film (for example, Alain Resnais' 1993 film version of Alan Ayckbourn's play *Smoking/No Smoking*), the technological challenge for creators of electronic interactive fiction was 'to find a way of turning imaginary worlds lodged in the writer's head into virtual worlds lodged in the computer's memory' (Woolley 1992: 155). The precedent was *Adventure*, a computerized version of role-playing games like Dungeons and Dragons, developed in the 1960s at Stanford University's Artificial Intelligence Laboratory.

Adventure and its descendants continued to evolve through the late 1970s, when interactive text games migrated from academic and corporate mainframes to home computers. There the form was married with popular fiction and role-playing games to produce a second generation of text adventures that retained the problem-solving design of the original *Adventure*. In the main, these games were not networks of possibilities to be explored, but arrangements of obstacles to be overcome in the progress to a determined goal. Later, in the 1980s, there emerged a third generation of interactive fiction in which the influence of game scenarios has been less noticeable – although, at the same time, the game scenario fictions have continued to thrive. The multiple fictions of the third generation are narrative networks capable of differing significantly on every reading. And with the advent of the Web, such fictions are able to exploit the new freedoms offered in terms of size, complexity and design.

The most effective techniques for achieving a strong storyline in the print medium are linearity, plot, characterization, textual coherence, resolution and closure. The same techniques can be used in the context of new media, as with movies on DVD and e-books, although their effectiveness can also be diminished in varying degrees. Writers using the new media, however, have played with the electronic medium's capacity to create open-ended stories with multiple narrative strands and have found alternative strategies and techniques for engaging readers' attention (Snyder 1996).

In one sense, each reading of an electronic narrative is a linear experience: confronted with one frame after another, readers are still aware of a narrative, however confused it may be. At the same time, the narrative seems to contain more than one voice and to change direction abruptly. Each electronic narrative handles in its own way the tension between the linearity of the reading experience and the multiplicity of electronic narrative.

According to Aristotle (1959), a narrative must have a beginning, a middle and an end. Electronic narratives, however, interrogate not only Aristotelian notions of beginning and end, but also his assumptions about the sequence of parts and the unity of the finished work. Electronic narrative calls into question some of the most basic points about plot and story in the Aristotelian tradition. By apparently dispensing with linear organization, linearity becomes a quality of readers' experience within single chunks of text and their experience of following particular paths. Although the experience of linearity does not disappear altogether, narrative chunks do not follow one another in a page turning, forward direction. In electronic narratives, space is multi-dimensional and theoretically infinite.

Electronic narratives also pose problems for traditional understandings of beginnings and endings. In traditional print narratives, beginnings imply endings and endings require some sort of formal and thematic closure. Literary convention decrees that endings must either satisfy or in some way respond to expectations raised during the reading of the narrative. Electronic narratives have taken a cautious approach to the problem of beginnings by offering readers a block of text labelled with something like 'start here', that combines the functions of title page, introduction and opening paragraph, perhaps reflecting the reluctance of some writers to disorientate readers at the point of their first contact with the narrative.

By avoiding the corresponding devices for achieving closure, however, such electronic narratives may challenge readers. It is up to readers to decide how, when and why the narrative finishes. Of course, we are not naive about unresolved texts. Print and cinematic narratives provide instances of multiple closure and also a combination of closure linked to new beginnings. The fact that twentieth-century writers and film makers frequently offer their audience little in the way of closure indicates that, as readers and writers, we have long learnt to live and read more open-endedly than discussions of narrative form may lead us to believe. However, culturally familiar though we are with the absence or denial of closure, we may still find the consequences disturbing.

Creating electronic narratives

There are several ways of thinking about how writers create electronic narratives. The first is to conceive of it as a hypertext. Hypertext provides a means of arranging information in a non-sequential manner with the computer automating the process of connecting one piece of information to another. Within a hypertext system, individual media objects (sound, photos, film, animation, graphics and so on) are wired together by hyperlinking. A hyperlink creates a connection between two elements. Elements connected through hyperlinks can exist on the same computer or on different computers connected on a network, such as the Web. Hypertext users get their own versions of the complete text by selecting pathways through the structure. They can create, manipulate and examine a network of nodes connected by relational links. Hypertext differs from printed text by offering users multiple paths through a body of information: it allows users to make their own connections and to produce their own meanings.

Manovich explains the processes of creating electronic narratives somewhat differently. For him, creating narrative work in new media can be understood as 'the construction of an interface to a database' (Manovich 2001: 226). The user of the narrative is traversing a database, following links between its records as established by the database's creator. Using this logic, an interactive narrative can be understood 'as the sum of multiple trajectories through a database' (Manovich: 227).

However, Manovich is also quick to point out that to qualify as a narrative, a cultural object has to satisfy a number of criteria. It should contain both an actor and a narrator; it should have three distinct levels consisting of the text, the story and the fabula; and its content should be a series of connected events caused or experienced by actors (Bal 1985).

Thus not all cultural objects are narratives. Just creating trajectories is not enough; the creator also has to control the semantics of the elements and the logic of their connections so that the resulting object will meet the criteria of narrative as outlined above. It also cannot be assumed that, by creating their own paths, users construct their own unique narratives.

The computer game that uses three-dimensional navigable space to visualize any kind of data – molecules, historical records, files in a computer, the Internet as a whole, the semantics of language – qualifies as a narrative. As with many computer games, the human experience of being in the world and the narrative itself are represented as continuous navigation through space.

Understanding the computerized database

From on the screen to behind the screen

When we think about the World Wide Web, it is most often in terms of what we see – on the screen. The notion of digital 'compositing' represents one way of explaining what we see when we look at the screen: the 'assembling together of a number of elements to create a single seamless object' (Manovich 2001: 139). As Walton (in press) explains: 'Like other new media, the Web is meant to be experienced as a seamless visual artefact, even though it is, in fact, assembled from a collection of files. In reality, the Web is only partially composited, with the seams of its construction more visible to users than is the case in many other new media.' But, for the purposes of Manovich's argument, it provides a useful way of thinking about what we see when we look at a computer screen.

We also need to know that what we see on the screen – those assemblages of different elements – is mediated by the visual interface. The Web human–computer interface describes the ways in which users interact with a computer. The interface includes physical input and output devices, such as the monitor, the keyboard and the mouse. It also includes the metaphors used to conceptualize the organization of computer data. For example, the Macintosh interface, which uses the metaphor of files and folders arranged on a desktop, has won the day, so to speak, as Microsoft has adopted the same icon-driven interface. As a result, the Macintosh office metaphor has become more or less ubiquitous.

Further, the visual interface includes ways of manipulating data: copy, rename and delete a file; list the contents of a directory; start and stop a program; set the computer's date and time (Manovich 2001). As more and more forms of culture become digitized, computer interfaces allow more interaction with cultural data: hence Manovich's notion of cultural interface. The language of cultural interfaces largely comprises elements of other, already familiar cultural forms, such as painting, photography and film.

As well as taking note of what is seen on the screen – the digital compositing and the visual interface – it is also salutary, argues Walton (in press), to consider some of the less visible aspects of the new Web texts. If we look 'behind the screen' of visual interfaces, 'we find the fundamental structures and architectures which underlie and accommodate the visual designs of the Web'. These structures may be less mesmerizing than the multimedia assemblages visible on the screen, but they are no less influential in determining what is communicated. For Walton, what goes on behind the screen is just as important as what is visible on it. When we look beyond the computer's visual surface and consider the assumptions embedded in the Web's underlying codes and conventions, we recognize that while the Web is a composited visual artefact, it is, using Manovich's definition, also a huge, chaotic database.

Database logic

Putting aside for the moment Manovich's (2001) claim that the database is not only a new cultural form but also the essence of new media in general, and of the Web in particular, a database represents an abstract process of organizing information. There are different types of databases – hierarchical, network, relational and object-oriented – and each uses a different model to organize data. But no matter how they are organized, databases appear to users as collections of items to view, navigate and search in a variety of ways. As such, the Web is structured according to what Manovich (2001: 215) calls 'database logic'.

The database logic of the Web provides us with ways of modelling the world through classifications and categorizations – perennially powerful ways of organizing knowledge, whether in electronic form or not. Walton points out that, although classification and categorization may not be as immediately engaging as other communicative forms, such as narrative, they are enabling systems which structure today's world in significant ways. As the logic of a classification is usually implicit, identifying that logic and learning to articulate its underlying assumptions, represent key skills for the current era. But, at the same time, Walton reminds us that the database 'provides users with reduced and simplified models of reality, which tend to homogenise and classify what they represent'.

The database as cultural form

The most familiar examples of the database form, in new media, are multimedia encyclopedias and other commercial CD-ROMS or DVDs that feature collections of things – recipes and photographs, for example. Multimedia works that have cultural content, such as the virtual tour through a museum collection, favour the database form. Instead of a con-structed narrative, the user is presented with a database of texts that can be navigated in a variety of ways. Another example is the CD-ROM devoted to a single cultural figure. Instead of a narrative biography, the user is presented with a database of images, video clips and texts that can be navigated in a variety of ways (Manovich 2001).

Where the form has really developed is in the context of the Internet. A Web page is a sequential list of separate elements: text blocks, images, video clips and links to other pages. It is always possible to add a new element to the list. In this sense, Web pages are collections of separate elements that are never complete: they can always grow. New elements can be added to the end of a list or they can be inserted anywhere in it. 'All this contributes to the anti-narrative logic of the Web. If new elements are being added over time, the result is a collection, not a story' (Manovich 2001: 221).

To users, databases appear as collections of items with which they can perform various operations – view, navigate, search. The experience of using such computerized collections of information, is quite distinct from reading a novel or watching a film. But, just as a literary or cinematic narrative presents a particular model of what a world is like, so too a data-base presents a particular model of what a particular world is like. In this sense, the database also represents an independent cultural form. It is what Manovich (2001: 219) calls 'a new symbolic form . . . a new way to structure our experience of ourselves and of the world'.

Regardless of whether new media objects present themselves as linear narratives, interactive narratives, databases or something else, underneath, on the level of material organization, they are all databases (Manovich). In new media, the database supports a variety of cultural forms that range from direct translation, that is, the database remains a database, to a form that is closer to a narrative. Overall, databases occupy a significant territory of the new media landscape.

Narrative and database: understanding the dynamics of their relationship

A number of questions posed by Manovich (2001) help to illuminate some key aspects of the dynamics of the relationship between narrative and database. First, do databases and narratives have the same status in computer culture? Although some media objects follow a database logic in their structure, whereas others do not, in general, 'creating a work in new media can be understood as the construction of an interface to a database' (Manovich 2001: 226). Manovich gives some examples. In the simplest case, the interface simply provides access to the underlying database. For instance, an image database can be represented as a page of miniature images; clicking on a miniature will retrieve the corresponding record. If a database is too large to display all its records, a search engine can allow the user to search for particular records. But the interface can also translate the underlying database into a very different experience. The example Manovich provides is Jeffrey Shaw's (1996) interactive installation *Legible City*, where the user navigates a virtual three-dimensional city composed from letters.

Thus, in new media, the database supports a variety of cultural forms that range from direct translation (that is, a database remains a database) to a form whose logic is the opposite of the logic of the material form itself – narrative. More precisely, a database can support narrative, but there is nothing in the logic of the form itself that would foster the generation of narrative.

In the computer age, the database becomes the centre of the creative process. According to Manovich (2001: 227): 'The new media object consists of one or more interfaces to a database of multimedia material.' He continues:

> If understood in this way, the user of a narrative is traversing a database, following links between its records as established by the database's creator. An interactive narrative . . . can be understood as the sum of multiple trajectories through a database.
>
> (Manovich: 227)

Second, in the context of new media, are these two cultural forms necessarily competing or oppositional? Manovich (2001: 233) says that he likes to think of them as 'two competing imaginations, two basic creative impulses, two essential responses to the world'. As he points out, the ancient Greeks produced long narratives but they also produced encyclopedias. The result of this competition to make meaning of the world is the production of hybrid forms. For example, it would be difficult to find an encyclopedia without a trace of narrative and vice versa.

Even if we resist naming it a competition, there exists a complex interplay and exchange between the two forms. For example, when users access a museum database, the objects in themselves are meaningless: they have to be framed in narrative terms to become meaningful. This might be achieved by a web developer or by the users, who create their own narratives as they choose which links to activate and, thus, which elements to juxtapose and connect.

Another example is located in new media design, which can be reduced to two basic approaches: constructing the right interface to a multimedia database or defining navigation methods through spatialized representations. The first approach is used in a website where the objective is to provide an interface to data and to give the user efficient access to information. The second is used in most computer games and virtual worlds where the aim is to psychologically immerse the user in an imaginary universe.

In general, these two goals represent the extremes of a continuum. Often, the two goals of information access and psychological engagement compete within the same new media object. A search engine tries to immerse the user in a universe in which the goal is to define, with increasing accuracy, the parameters of the quest. And in a game, there is a strong information processing dimension. Gathering clues and treasures, and updating a mental map of the universe of the game, align playing a computer game with other information processing tasks typical of computer culture. For example searching the Internet, scanning news groups, pulling records from a database, using a spreadsheet or data mining large data stores (Manovich 2001).

The third question is to do with the history of culture. Does the pre-eminence of the database form represent a break with the past so monumental that the new media will completely replace narrative with database? As Manovich (2001: 229) argues: 'New media does not radically break with the past; rather, it distributes weight differently between the categories that hold culture together, foregrounding what was in the background, and vice versa.' Radical breaks do not generally involve complete change, but a restructuration.

Taking meaning

We require an education in literature . . . in order to discover that what we assumed – with the complicity of our teachers – was nature is in fact culture, that what was given is no more than a way of taking.

(Howard 1992: vii)

In her now classic article, 'What no bedtime story means', Shirley Brice Heath (1982) argues that the culture children learn as they grow up is, in fact, ways of taking meaning from the environment around them. Even though making sense from books and relating their content to knowledge about the real world is only one way of taking meaning, it is often interpreted as 'natural' rather than learnt. However, taking meaning from books, says Heath, is as much a part of learnt behaviour as are ways of eating, sitting, playing games and building houses.

Twenty or so years later, at the beginning of the twenty-first century, we can apply the same logic to a different set of circumstances and for a different purpose. Today, just as in the 1980s, the culture that young people learn as they grow up is embodied in ways of taking meaning from the environment in which they are immersed. What has changed, however, is the nature of the environment. Young people continue to take meaning from stories printed in books, which of course, represents just one way of taking meaning. But they also have to make sense of screen-based, digital texts, located on the Web, and relate their form and content to knowledge about the real world. This represents another way of taking meaning.

As argued in this chapter, the form and content of these screen-based texts are different from their print counterparts: most are not based on the familiar narrative structure that has become both privileged and naturalized in our book-orientated culture. The dominant structure, indeed cultural form, in the context of the Web, is the database. Unlike narrative, it is in no danger of becoming naturalized: strangely, the cultural significance of the database has been largely overlooked.

As book-orientated teachers and their students interact in classrooms, the adults provide their students, through modelling and specific instruction, ways of taking from books, which seem natural in school and in numerous other social and institutional settings. These mainstream ways persist in formal education systems designed to prepare students for participation in settings involving book literacy. But book literacy, with its deep attachment to narrative as a hallowed cultural form, is now just one of the many literacies that students require to participate effectively in post-school settings. In particular, as this chapter has argued, students need opportunities in their classrooms to learn how to take meaning not just from the most familiar cultural forms but also from other, increasingly significant ones, such as the computerized database.

If the modern age provided people with robust narratives and modest amounts of information, today in the computer age we have too much information and too few narratives that can make sense of it all. Whether we like it or not, information access has become a central activity of the computer age. Information access is no longer just integral to the world of work, it is also a key category of culture. As such, it demands that we deal with it theoretically, pedagogically and aesthetically.

Note

The author thanks Marion Walton, University of Cape Town, for her generative response to an earlier version of this chapter.

References

Aristotle (1959) *The Poetics*, trans. L.J. Potts, *Aristotle on the Art of Fiction: An English Translation of Aristotle's Poetics with an introductory essay and explanatory notes.* Cambridge: Cambridge University Press.

Bal, M. (1985) *Narratology: Introduction to the Theory of Narrative.* Toronto: University of Toronto Press.

Borges, J.L. (1970) *Labyrinths*, D.A. Yates and J.E. Irby (eds). Harmondsworth: Penguin.

Cortazar, J. (1966) *Hopscotch*, trans. G. Rabassa. London: Collins Harvill.

Hardy, B. (1977) Narrative as a primary act of mind, in M. Meek, A. Warlow and G. Barton (eds) *The Cool Web: The Patterns of Children's Reading.* London: The Bodley Head.

Heath, S.B. (1982) What no bedtime story means: narrative skill at home and school, *Language and Society*, 11: 49–76.

Howard, R. (1992) A note on *S/Z*. Preface to R. Barthes, *S/Z*, trans. R. Miller. Oxford: Blackwell.

Manovich, L. (2001) *The Language of New Media.* Cambridge, MA: MIT Press.

Shaw, J. (1996) *Legible City.* Available at http://artnetweb.com/guggenheim/mediascape/shaw.html (accessed 22 February 2003).

Snyder, I. (1996) *Hypertext: The Electronic Labyrinth.* Melbourne: Melbourne University Press.

Walton, M. (in press) Behind the screen: the language of Web design, in I. Snyder and C. Beavis (eds) *Doing Literacy Online: Teaching, Learning and Playing in an Electronic World.* Cresskill, NJ: Hampton Press.

Williams, R. (1976) *Keywords: A Vocabulary of Culture and Society.* London: Fontana.

Woolley, B. (1992) *Virtual Worlds: A journey in Hype and Hyperreality.* Harmondsworth: Penguin.

6

CONSTRUCTING (AND DECONSTRUCTING) READING THROUGH HYPERTEXT: LITERATURE AND THE NEW MEDIA

Teresa M. Dobson

In the preceding chapter, Ilana Snyder discussed the reconception of narrative theory in new media contexts, from text-based adventure games to hyperfiction. Such genres, she observes, challenge conventional notions of literary structure by confounding reader expectations in terms of linearity, coherence, closure and so on. As Snyder intimates, much has been written about the implications of electronic narratives for literary theory. Indeed, the excitement with which interactive fiction was received by the first wave of hypertext theorists (Lanham 1993; Landow 1997; Bolter 2001) had largely to do with the ways in which the genre made explicit ideas about textuality central to post-structuralist literary theory. In this chapter, I wish to consider briefly this connection between literary theory and new technologies for writing by discussing (1) how literary reading processes are modified and extended in new media environments, and (2) how English teachers might invite their students into meaningful explorations of, and interactions with/in, such environments.

Before I proceed, however, I should say that I use the term 'hypertext' to refer to interconnected computer-based texts that may be read in a variety of sequences and that may incorporate multiple media. I conceive of *text*, then, broadly as anything that might be *read* (that is, interpreted), such as words, images, animations, film, and therefore do not wish to make a distinction between hypertext and hypermedia. In this understanding I concur with (while extending to include animation and sound) the definition of hypertext first put forward by Nelson (1965: 96): 'a body of written or pictorial material interconnected in such a complex way that it could not conveniently be presented or represented on paper'. The middle component of this early definition is also key to my own understanding: hypertext should exhibit a complexity of interconnection that affords readers multiple paths. Thus, not all electronic texts are hypertextual; conversely, and to take issue with Nelson, not all hypertexts are electronic. (Aarseth (1997: 1 ff.) makes a similar argument, presenting multiple examples in codex and other forms of what he terms 'ergodic' literature, or literature in which 'nontrivial effort' is required to traverse the text. Bolter (2001: 138 ff.) likewise presents a brief history of non-electronic precursors of hypertext.

Hypertext has had many incarnations in the past decades. Early examples (informational or literary) consisting largely of networked prose or poetry have been succeeded by those that increasingly employ a variety of media, including a growing body of aesthetic texts that marry literary arts and interactive media (see, for example, http://www.digitalfiction.co.uk/ and http://www.bornmagazine.org/). Clearly it would not be possible to posit a theory of reading that would account for how readers engage with the wide range of forms currently represented in cyberspace. What I attempt to do here, rather, is to provide a sense of some of the more common issues that have arisen in discussions of electronic literature and reading, to present some findings from a study with readers of literature presented in electronic form, and to connect these discussions to secondary English teaching practices. Before continuing, readers who are not familiar with the genre may wish to examine some of the hypertexts available in the Eastgate Reading Room (http://www.eastgate.com/ReadingRoom.html). The selection offered there provides a sense of the range of types and patterns. More innovative use of media may be observed, as noted above, at *Digital Fiction* and *Born Magazine*.

Hypertext and literary theory

To situate this chapter theoretically, it is worth taking a moment to pursue the notion raised above of how hypertext has been associated with post-structuralism. Much has been written on this topic, and what I present here constitutes only a nod in the direction of that literature. (For those interested in pursuing this subject further, Snyder's (1996) book *Hypertext: The Electronic Labyrinth* is a good place to start; alternatively, Landow's (1997) *Hypertext 2.0: The Convergence of Contemporary Critical Theory and Technology* is one of the key early volumes on this topic.) Briefly, then, and by way of definition, post-structuralism is a branch of critical textual analysis that extends and critiques the tenets of structuralism. While structuralists conceive of language as a clearly demarcated structure composed of elements at various phonological, grammatical and semantic levels, post-structuralists emphasize the instability and plurality of meaning (*OED*). Such an emphasis challenges, among other things, the structuralist tendency to 'treat individual texts as discrete, closed-off entities and to focus exclusively on internal structures' (Chandler 2002: 194). Thus, as Eagleton (1983: 129) observes, language envisaged by post-structuralists begins to look 'like a sprawling limitless web where there is a constant interchange and circulation of elements, where none of the elements is absolutely definable and where everything is caught up and traced through by everything else'.

Considering Eagleton's descriptors in the preceding statement ('limitless', 'web', 'interchange' and so on) gives a sense of why hypertextual writing spaces have sparked such interest among literary theorists. Viewed from the perspective of print technology, which emphasizes the discrete (that is, bound) work and has tended to privilege continuity, ideas that are key to post-structural semiotics, such as fragmentation, non-linearity and intertextuality are difficult to conceptualize. In the mid-1970s, for example, Barthes (1974: 13) proposed that we should 'star' the text, cutting it up into a series of 'brief, contiguous fragments'; Derrida (1976: 87), pursuing a similar idea, claimed that we must seek a different organization of textual space – one that is 'without the line'. Shortly thereafter, Kristeva (1986), drawing on the work of Bakhtin (1984), challenged the notion of the discrete work, arguing instead for the construal of the 'literary word' as '*an intersection of textual surfaces* rather than a *point*', and emphasizing that 'any text is constructed as a mosaic of quotations' (Kristeva 1986: 36–7; emphasis in original). As Bolter suggests ideas, such as these, which are difficult when presented through print to audiences whose understandings of what it means to read and write are grounded in print-based notions of literature and literacy, are 'simplified in and through electronic media' because they can be *shown* (Bolter 2001: 151). Hypertext, particularly when constructed as a highly networked series of short nodes connected by links, may be construed as exemplifying the fragmentation of which Barthes speaks, affording the different organization of textual space called for by Derrida, and elucidating Kristeva's notions of intertextuality. Thus Landow (1997: 2) premises his book on the notion that the medium has provided a laboratory in which theorists might test their ideas about literature and reading.

Electronic media and the changing roles of the reader/writer

Pursuing this connection between post-structuralism and hypertext, early discussions of the new media from the perspective of literary theory devote much time to a consideration of how reader and writer roles are modified in fragmentary, non-linear, unbounded writing spaces. Such discussions not infrequently propose that engaging with networked computer-based texts requires more activity on the part of the reader, and conclude that the technology is destined to improve the experience of literary reading. For example, noting the roots of electronic literature in computerized, text-based, adventure games, Bolter (2001: 126 ff.) highlights the game-like quality of textual spaces where reader-players fashion documents by choosing their own paths. Elsewhere, he argues that electronic texts are like scripts or musical scores that readers must enact:

> The reader performs the text, perhaps only for himself or herself, perhaps for another reader, who may then choose to perform the first reader's text for others. In this way electronic writing can serve to define new levels of creativity that fall between the apparent originality of the romantic artist and the apparent passivity of the traditional reader.
>
> (Bolter 2001: 173)

Douglas (2000: 23), following a similar line of thought, calls on the metaphor of dance: 'a work of hypertext fiction can act as a blueprint for a series of potential interactions, and your movements through it, a dance choreographed by an absent author who has anticipated the questions, needs, and whims of imaginary readers'.

Of course, according to certain schools of thought, readers have always been active, or 'players', because they necessarily reconstruct texts within their own worldviews by reading themselves into narratives, drawing inferences in order to fill in temporal, spatial or causal gaps and so on (Rosenblatt 1968; Iser 1978); and yet, clearly hypertext extends such processes in important ways. Readers of interactive fiction, for example, must do more than reconstruct a narrative that exists in a predetermined order: they must engage in an activity of construction *and* reconstruction, both determining the storyline *and* filling perceived gaps in meaning with their own imagined narratives. The result, according to Landow (1997: 90), is 'an active, even intrusive reader' who feels a sense of agency because the hypertext writing space has infringed 'upon the power of the writer, removing some of it and granting that portion to the reader'. Presumably this agency is further extended in interactive, or 'constructive' (Joyce 1988), hypertexts that afford readers opportunity to join in the game of authoring by adding their own nodes and links, leading Landow (1994: 14) to coin a new term for the act of engaging with electronic texts: 'wreading'.

Although arguments such as these afford some interesting points of departure for considering potential classroom applications, their limitations have been remarked upon by a number of critics. Miall (1999), for example, argues that liberationist statements about the supposed autonomy offered readers by hypertextual structures have trivialized the serious question of how reading processes do change in such environments. He takes issue, in particular, with the notion that structural linearity is constraining, arguing instead, that multi-directional organizations may in fact be antipathetic to the sort of deep reflection that characterizes literary response. Determining the veracity of this hypothesis, he submits, would require that researchers move beyond theorizing and begin, instead, to put their claims to the test with actual readers. This assessment is echoed by Douglas (2000: 73), who likewise calls for studies with readers, not from the perspective of interface design and software engineering, but from the perspective of 'how hypertext may transform the way we read or write texts and, indeed, our whole conception of a satisfactory reading experience' (Douglas). In other words, she calls for reader-response studies with electronic literature.

Some years after the publication of Miall's and Douglas's statements, however, such research is still uncommon: empirical studies tend to involve task-orientated work with informational hypertexts, such as electronic encyclopedias, and discussions of reading literary, hypertexts tend to be largely theoretical. Aarseth (1997: 14) points to two further problems with hypertext theorizing: (1) the tendency to apply theories of literary criticism to new media 'without any reassessment of the terms and concepts involved', and (2) the related but reverse tendency to describe the new media as 'radically different from the old, with attributes solely determined by the material technology of the medium'. Aarseth thus argues for careful scholarship around reception of digital texts that takes account of both their distinctness from and likeness to previous forms. Ultimately, discussions of whether hypertext improves literary reading, as it is understood in the context of print, or whether the medium elucidates textual criticism written in response to print genres are not particularly helpful, for they fail to take account of the unique features of the new media.

Electronic literature and the experience of reading: a study

Having remarked upon the predominance of theory over empirical research on the question of hypertext and literary reading and considering the focus of this chapter on ICT and the secondary English curriculum, I am mindful of the need to bring this discussion to a consideration: (1) of how young adults engage with hypertext, and (2) of what implications this might have for the teaching of English. To undertake the first of these tasks, I wish to draw on data gleaned through a study of my own with young adult readers of literature presented in electronic form.

Participants in this study were 60 first-year undergraduate students mostly under the age of 20. The students had declared a variety of majors, mostly in the arts and sciences, but otherwise were a fairly homogeneous group: all were enrolled in a first-year psychology course at a Canadian university in an urban centre of moderate size (800,000), all were native speakers of English or ESL speakers with several years' English immersion, and 88 per cent were female, reflecting the demographics of psychology classes at the post-secondary institution in question. Most of the participants were in their thirteenth year of study (formal secondary education ends at Year 12 in most Canadian provinces, while bachelor degrees are four years long.)

The study entailed the manipulation of a modernist short story for electronic media. The narrative in question, Sean O'Faolain's 'The Trout' (O'Faolain 1980), is a brief text (approximately 1,500 words) bearing the stylistic markers of the fairy tale. It is replete with simple, almost childlike, constructions that at times belie the complexity of the narrative. Twelve-year-old Julia is portrayed as a precocious girl who is beginning to question her parents' moralistic responses to her queries about the world. While exploring the wooded garden of her family's summer retreat, she discovers a well and trapped within a small pool of evaporating water, a live trout. Distressed by its predicament and by the indifference of those around her, she plans and executes the trout's rescue. Her midnight action constitutes a rite of passage that, the story implies, frees her from the gullibility of early childhood years.

This narrative was presented to readers on computer as a series of ten nodes. It consisted of alphabetic text alone; no sound or visual media were added. To proceed through the narrative, members of a control group (prefixed 'L' – linear) activated a 'next' link positioned at the bottom of each node; the experimental group (prefixed 'S' – simulation) were required to choose from among three embedded links in order to proceed, a scenario which led them to believe that the text was multi-directional even though it was not (see Figures 6.1 and 6.2). Readers were asked to comment after the fact about anything that struck them about the reading experience, in terms, both of the content and of the presentation of the text. Transcribed reader commentaries were coded exhaustively for different features, or constituents, of experience. Altogether, 76 features were

---

This year she had the extra joy of showing it to her small brother, and of terrifying him as well as herself. And for him the fear lasted longer because his legs were so short and she had gone out at the far end while he was still screaming and racing.

Next

Figure 6.1 A node of 'The Trout' presented in linear form

> This year she had the <u>extra joy</u> of showing it to her small <u>brother</u>, and of terrifying him as well as herself. And for him the fear lasted longer because his legs were so short and she had gone out at the far end while he was still <u>screaming and racing</u>.

Figure 6.2   A node of 'The Trout' presented in simulated hypertext form

identified, and these were divided into ten categories of response. For the purpose of this chapter I will focus on trends evidenced within four categories of response, given their potential for enlightening the question of how modifications in literary reading processes, elicited by electronic forms, inform the project of teaching school English. The categories are: (1) story and structure, (2) interpretive and observational, (3) imagery and visualization, and (4) response to style (see Table 6.1).

Before continuing, I should note that there are two obvious limitations to the study design. First, the texts used are not native to the electronic medium, and second, the simulated hypertext prevents readers from engaging in activities that are an essential component of hypertext reading, such as revisiting key nodes in the course of making repeated passes through a network (Joyce 1988). With respect to the first, hypertext theorists would argue that the method is procrustean at best; how, after all, are we to approach an understanding of the ways in which hypertext modifies reader strategies, if we undertake studies involving manipulation of texts written for a different medium? This in fact has been the chief criticism of reader-response research conducted with (or, more to the point, without) hypertext (Bernstein 1997). Certainly this criticism is valid: in spite of its guise, 'The Trout' lacks many of the defining features of literary hypertext, such as randomness, ironic juxtapositioning, repetition effected through cyclical structures, the lack of a definitive ending and so on. In short, the

Table 6.1 Categories of response discussed in this paper

Category	Description
1. Story and structure	Response to structure, plot, suspense, etc.
2. Interpretive and observational	Interpretation (e.g. on a thematic or symbolic level)
	Observation (e.g. notes presence of allusion, identifies the protagonist, etc.)
3. Imagery and visualization	Remarks upon imagery; speaks of being able to visualize the setting (often these two were paired)
4. Response to style	Response to style (e.g. notes and responds to stylistically foregrounded language)

text's transitional cues belie its true nature and this in itself has the potential to set reader expectations inappropriately. Further, and with respect to the second criticism, in a highly networked environment readers may browse extensively, or loop, through a series of nodes repeatedly in the course of their reading. They may back up, revisit a node multiple times from different viewpoints and so on. It is unlikely that any two readers will pass through the nodes in the same order or even, in some cases, that they will encounter much of the same material in the course of exploring the same text. Clearly this indeterminacy is an integral part of reading some (but not all) hypertexts and choosing not to allow readers such freedom, necessarily closes off certain avenues of exploration with respect to determining the nature of reader response to the new medium. Simultaneously, however, other avenues of investigation are opened, and these yield information that is important in its own right. The simulation design was devised in an effort to ensure that all participants read the same material in the same sequence, in order to get at the following question: How might having a *sense* of multi-directionality modify affective response to literature?

Responding to 'The Trout': 'Story and structure'

Comments made by readers of the simulation demonstrated that the design did have the desired effect: all readers believed they were reading a multi-directional text and that the choices they made between links were affecting the path of the narrative. Therefore, although the simulation was not a true hypertext, the study does have the potential to illuminate the question of how readers experience multi-directional electronic literature.

As a general observation with respect to trends evidenced in the data, participants who read the simulation had difficulty with the text. They were far more likely, for instance, to express confusion (Confuse), to remark that the story seemed incomplete (Loss), or to complain that the narrative was disjointed (Story flow–) (see Table 6.2). Given that there was no difference between the texts presented to readers in each group other than the placement of links, the disparity between the two groups on this count was remarkable, demonstrating, if nothing else, the extent to which readers' perceptions of their reading environment may modify their understanding of content. Consider, by way of example, the following remark by a simulation reader:

> There were bits and pieces . . . it made it a little difficult sometimes to fill in the gaps. It almost seemed like there were bits of information that were missing, but I was able to put the puzzle together, so to speak, was able to figure out what was going on just from the action and the dialogue in the story.
>
> (S113)

Table 6.2 Frequency of category 1 feature occurrence

	Linear		Simulation	
	Total	Protocols	Total	Protocols
Confuse	4	3	11	6
Loss	0	0	13	9
Story flow–	2	2	15	9
Story+	7	6	1	1
Story–	5	3	6	5
Storyq	0	0	16	8

Comments such as this, in which readers expressed the feeling that they had missed portions of the text, were made by simulation readers only (see the Loss feature in Table 6.2) and suggested a rather interesting effect of the presentation of that text. Evidently the presence of embedded links drew readers attention to rifts in the temporal, spatial or causal continuity of the narrative. As Iser (1978) has noted, such rifts exist in all narratives and reading therefore entails a continuous process of filling in gaps. Unless the text is disjointed in the extreme, we engage in this process unconsciously, making sense of narrative by drawing inferences that account for natural breaks in continuity. For example, if a character is described knocking on a front door at one moment and standing in a kitchen the next, we might account for the shift by presuming that she has been admitted to the home and invited to the kitchen. Readers in the control group appeared to engage in this form of reading activity unconsciously, accounting for shifts in the narrative between the exterior and interior settings, and making no remark that they found 'The Trout' difficult to follow. On the contrary, the simulation readers seemed to become overly attuned to the gaps in the narrative – to the point, apparently, that this attunement at times interfered with the reading process.

In spite of his initial difficulties, however, it is noteworthy that the reader (cited above) ultimately embraced the challenge presented to him. His description of his reading strategy calls to mind that presented by Moulthrop (1991) in his assessment of the strategies employed by students working with a hypertext adaptation of Borges' 'Garden of Forking Paths' (Douglas 2000). Moulthrop suggests, in particular, that readers of the Borges adaptation engaged in an interesting inversion of the reading process as described by Brooks (1984): rather than reading for plot, they plotted their readings. The above reader, similarly, treated the story as if it were a puzzle to be solved – successful sleuthing beneath the table for the mandatory misplaced pieces was merely part of the game. Thus, after stating that he had difficulty following the narrative because bits of the text appeared to be lost, he hastened to add that he overcame this problem through perseverance: 'but I was able to put the puzzle together, so to speak, and was able to figure out what was going on just from the action and the dialogue in the story' (S113). Noteworthy in this response is that he apparently does not 'find' his misplaced pieces, but instead infers what is not there from what is. This reading process approximates that described by Iser (1978): those inevitable spaces in the logical sequence of the narrative into which we read our own understandings are, at least in part, what allow us to engage in personally meaningful interactions with literary texts. S113's response is remarkable, then, not because he engages in the process of inference – something that all readers must do – but because he recognizes that this is what he is doing.

One effect of the way in which the simulation made explicit the structure of the text, is that it may have made some readers more cognizant of the essential discontinuity of narrative and of their own involvement in constructing it in the process of reading, a scenario which would support the claims of early hypertext theorists such as Johnson-Eilola (1993: 383):

> More than any previous text technology, hypertext encourages both writers and readers – roles we might now provisionally combine under the label of hypertext 'writer/readers' – to confront and work consciously and concretely with deconstruction, intertextuality, the decentering of the author, and the reader's complicity with the construction of the text.

Informing the text: 'Interpretive and observational'

It is worth noting that the response of reader S113 was echoed by a number of participants in the study. Consider, by way of example, the following remarks made by two female readers:

> Reading this story off the computer was kind of confusing at first because as I went to different screens I realized the story wasn't in order, so I had to get pieces, bits and pieces of information from, in different order. And it was kind of confusing at first, but then I just adapted, and learnt to take the information as it was coming, and then pieced it all together at the end.
>
> (S305)

> The story was kind of, actually kind of confusing for me. I really didn't get all that much . . . I got bits and parts of it, about the fish, and how she wanted to let it go, but it didn't really, this story didn't really strike me, so I didn't really have much feeling . . . The story seemed kind of

choppy, kind of incoherent . . . it would jump from one topic to another
topic about her and her brother fighting, and with the fish disappearing.
I just couldn't get it.

(S323)

The descriptors used by these two readers, as well as S113's comment,
cited earlier, are surprisingly similar: 'bits and pieces', 'information', 'putting (or piecing) it all together'. The first reader (S113) is pleased that he is
able to 'figure it out', and the second that she is able to 'adapt', but the last
cannot connect the seemingly disjointed 'bits' or 'topics' and rejects the
experience at least in part because it fails to evoke feeling. It would seem
that the first two commentaries paint a fair picture of the reality of reading
at the current historical moment: texts are transforming and readers are
adapting. Undoubtedly replicating this study in ten, even five, years time
would yield different results. Perhaps, given further exposure to literature
in electronic form, the last reader might also 'figure it out'. But the understanding that text technologies and reading processes are changing does
not make irrelevant the exercise of examining how readers are experi-
encing this change, or of considering what the nature of the change
might be.

The use of the term 'information' in the above statements seems particularly suggestive with respect to these last two points. The employment of
this term as a descriptor for the narrative occurred a number of times in
both conditions and generally signalled a distancing from the text on a
personal level, as evidenced in the following remark by a daily Internet
and email user, who nevertheless did not enjoy reading 'The Trout' on
computer: 'It didn't seem like I was actually reading a story. It seemed like I
was reading some sort of information thing on the computer. Also, it was
really hard for me to visualize and for this to actually seem realistic' (S325).
Simulation readers were more than twice as likely as linear (control group)
readers to describe the narrative as 'information' (linear 3; simulation 8),
suggesting that the presentation mode appeared to modify, at some level,
readers' sense of genre. They were also more likely to note that they felt
distanced from the text because of the medium (linear 11; simulation 19),
suggesting that there may have been some conflation in readers minds of
the formal properties of the text (that is, with or without embedded
links) and the computer medium itself. The following excerpt from one
reader's commentary gives interesting insight as to what factors may have
contributed to such feelings:

Reading this text on a computer versus on a book, or in a book, I should
say, it kind of separated me a little bit because I was more aware of the
environment, or my environment . . . a computer is sort of an entity on
its own, as if it's holding the text a bit aloof from you. You can read it,
but you can't quite get into it as much. I was more me, and less the girl,

than I would have been in a book, I think. Choosing between the links was also very frustrating. I didn't like that because I had this feeling all the way through that there was something else going on, other stories, or other details, or other information that I didn't get to read, and I don't know how that would have – if – I didn't know if that would have affected the story, or my perception of the story.

(S327)

There is more to the estrangement exhibited here than mere aversion to the computer as a vehicle for literary text, due to inexperience with the medium. Participant S327 has a nagging sense that she is missing portions of the story, elaborating at some length:

Making all those choices – every one seemed to sort of compound the loss of the last one. If I had . . . three choices in just about every one, I missed two every time, and after three choices, I'd missed a good six links . . . I felt like I'd missed a lot of the story, or a lot of the background, or a lot of the details. I mean, it made sense as it was, but it's sort of like a book where you get to the end and you want a sequel just to hear about the other characters that were sort of mentioned but never really explored. Except in this case it was like the sequel was written but the only place you could get it is some library half way across the continent.

(S327)

In the case of this study, such responses might be attributed in a large degree to the lack of a back button in the simulation, but I am not willing to attribute the reaction solely to the study design, for I have observed similar responses among readers in my current study who are working with a number of native electronic texts, including *Patchwork Girl* (Jackson 1995) and *My Body* (Jackson 1997). Ultimately, readers of large-scale multi-directional hyperfiction often struggle not only to determine their location in the network but also to determine what they have read and what remains to be read. Their efforts to map their readings in complicated networks (Moulthrop 1991), or to find a route through the maze (Douglas 2000), or to solve the puzzle (my own readers' description), are all attempts at ordering – as is the above reader's desire to see everything laid out squarely so that she might confirm that she has explored all there is to explore.

Douglas (2000: 83 ff.) has considered the question of closure in hyperfiction, resolving (like Joyce 1988) that hypertext demands re-reading, and that arriving at closure in this medium is a matter of exhausting possibilities. Perhaps this is so, but a question not addressed in this assessment is what aspect of literary response (if any) is replaced by activities, such as mapping, finding, solving, exploring and ordering? The results of this study suggest that one side effect of diverting reader attention to matters of structure is a recasting of literary text as *information* – a not surprising turn of events given the derivation of the term: literally, *in-form*, 'to put into proper form or order, to arrange; to compose (a writing)' (*OED*). As one reader puts it: 'I chose links that sort of related to each other because I thought, you know, that way I'd get the most information out of it, and I'd have the most continuity' (S304). I do not wish to construe this as an altogether negative thing, for it is clear that this exercise prompted some interesting critical reading strategies. For example, a feature of response peculiar to simulation readers was the tendency to question the plausibility of the narrative, and to puzzle over whether their efforts to 'in-form' the text had achieved the best results (see Table 7.1, Storyq). For example, one reader wondered if the narrative she 'ended up with' was 'appropriate'; another voiced her concern about the possibility of choosing 'wrong' links; and a third reflected that his choices were wanting because he had failed to discover basic information about the characters:

> I chose, I don't know, not a series of links that would have been, I don't know, appropriate.
>
> (S301)

> I felt a little, like, self-conscious about choosing links for fear that I would miss something else, or choose the wrong one.
>
> (S325)

> At one point I kind of wished I had chosen to learn more about the characters in the story because near the end I found myself wondering who was who exactly.
>
> (S328)

Conversely, some readers were pleased because they surmised they had in fact chosen 'suitable' links, which they described as those that lead to 'the next part of the story' (S310) or that effected a 'normal' (S305) or (in the case of the following reader) 'proper' progression of the narrative:

> When I chose Julia at the very beginning, I just felt like that was a proper opening because, you know, at the beginning – at the introduction of a story – you learn a little bit about the characters, and just what they're doing and stuff before they get into real action, and description, and plot.
>
> (S304)

In other words, the simulation may have encouraged a more critical mode of reading because readers in this condition did not take the plot for granted, as did those who read the linear version. Instead, they brought their understandings of possible narrative sequences to bear on the question of what might constitute an appropriate order of events in the case of 'The Trout'. While their awareness of possible narrative sequences, as evidenced in their commentaries was clearly very limited, having been gleaned from what they had encountered most in their reading lives (conventional western fiction in print), the finding tends to support, again, claims that hypertext may encourage a particular level of meta-cognitive awareness among readers with respect to their reading processes and as well, a level of critical awareness with respect to narrative structure and substance.

Certainly the simulation appeared to have no effect on students' ability to engage in the sorts of traditional analysis commonly undertaken in literature classrooms, as evidenced by the occurrence of features in Category 2, interpretive and observational. Comments in this cluster reflected in many ways the formal literary training of the group participating in the study, and included remarks about language, theme and symbolism, as well as the identification of allusion and so on. For example, one reader mused about whether 'The Trout' is a 'coming of age' story (S302), and another raised the possibility that Julia is 'the saviour' of the fish (S321). Such comments represent the readers' efforts to contextualize the story within their own frameworks of literary knowledge (that is, the first categorizes the story as belonging to a genre with which she is clearly familiar, and the second determines which archetypal role might best fit Julia). The total occurrence of features in this category was remarkably similar in both groups of readers (linear 52; simulation 54). The difference in presentation mode, thus, appeared to have little effect on readers' tendencies or abilities to engage in literary analysis, suggesting that electronic texts with unusual structures are as likely as other forms to encourage critical modes of literary engagement that are congruent with curricular goals in secondary English classrooms.

The inward eye/I: 'Imagery and visualization' and 'Response to style'

Before I sum up my discussion of reader response, I should comment briefly on the two further categories in which significant differences between the participant groups were revealed: 'Imagery and visualization' and 'Response to style' (see Table 6.3).

The first of these categories included instances of reader response to imagery and stylistic foregrounding, and the second concerned features of response reflecting personal involvement in the text. With respect to the first of these, interestingly, the control group tended to comment more frequently on the unifying imagery of the narrative, making remarks such as the following: 'I liked the imagery at the beginning of the story. It let me visualize the scene in my mind.' Conversely, simulation readers tended to remark more frequently on localized instances of stylistic foregrounding (for example alliteration, metaphor, personification), as well as on the way in which this sort of language transformed their understandings of particular constructs (see Table 6.3). Consider, for example, the following remark:

> The phrase, moon mice on the water, I have no idea what exactly that means. I can't figure out how to tie in mice with the moon unless it's something to do with the moon being full of cheese, but I really like that phrase. It, it, I guess partially because it was something different – I mean, you don't normally connect mice with the moon. That made me stop at it and go, *whoa* – which was odd, especially since that was a section where I was speeding right along trying to find out exactly what would happen.
>
> (S327)

This reader's engagement with the text is clearly transformative, in that it has led her to reconceptualize how things she had heretofore regarded as disconnected might, in fact, be connected. In terms of literary response, this is an instance of what Miall and Kuiken (1994) have termed 'defamiliarization' (a moment in which the familiar is made unfamiliar), and signals a high degree of attention to particular, stylistically rich local structures. Of all participants in the study, this reader was particularly attuned to foregrounding even to the extent that the language of her own commentary at times echoed that of foregrounded passages in the text. She spoke, for example, of 'little scraps of phrases' that caught her eye, an apparently involuntary repetition of a description of a path through the forest, which at night, is 'full of little scraps of moon' (O'Faolain 1980: 386). The reversal between groups of instances of commentary on defamiliarization and foregrounding versus imagery and visualization, suggests that possibly because simulation readers struggled at some level to make sense of the text, their attention was diverted to surface features; or put differently, they shifted focus from global to local textual structures.

This understanding is again supported by the early results of my current study with readers of native hypertext. One reader in this study, for example, remarked that she initially began reading *Patchwork Girl* with the

Table 6.3 Frequency of categories 3 and 4 feature occurrence

	Linear		Simulation	
	Total	Protocols	Total	Protocols
Foregrounding	4	3	11	6
Defamiliarization	3	3	12	5
Imagery	22	16	14	7
Visual	10	8	6	4

object of making sense of a 'story', but when she happened upon the node 'all written' early in her reading, she modified her strategy, resolving instead, to read individual nodes for the merits of the language and notions therein, and not to persist in the activity of constructing a narrative. The node to which she refers begins as follows:

> Assembling these patched words in an electronic space, I feel half-blind, as if the entire text is within reach, but because of some myopic condition I am only familiar with from dreams, I can see only that part most immediately before me, and have no sense of how that part relates to the rest. When I open a book I know where I am, which is restful. My reading is spatial and even volumetric. I tell myself, I am a third of the way down through a rectangular solid, I am a quarter of the way down the page, I am here on the page, here on this line, here, here, here. But where am I now? I am in a here and a present moment that has no history and no expectations for the future.
>
> (all written)

The reader, having alluded to this node as a pivotal point in her reading, remarked that it was only when she began reading for 'the present moment', in accordance with the suggestion offered in 'all written', that she began to enjoy the reading experience. Her revelation recalls a notion mentioned earlier in the chapter: that is, rather than looking at what electronic literature is not doing (that is, engaging students in the sort of reading strategies we might expect of novel readers), we would do well to consider what reading strategies it does promote and consider how those strategies might inform the activity of teaching literature.

Implications for practice

What, then, are the possibilities for electronic literature in English classrooms? First, and to return to the theory section at the outset of this chapter, reading avant-garde literary texts, electronic or otherwise, encourages students to challenge conventional (generally Aristotelian) notions of literary structure that predominate in many literature classrooms. This scenario goes both ways of course: the presentation of a non-conforming example may also be used as a catalyst for discussion of established conventions. Second, interacting with such literature brings readers to an awareness of their own reading processes. The challenges faced by hypertext readers need not be viewed merely as products of an awkward literary form: they may be viewed, rather, as openings for discussion about reading strategies. As noted earlier, activities (such as accounting for gaps in continuity) are common to all forms of reading: hypertext offers teachers an excellent opportunity to demonstrate this reality and to take

up, as well, the question of how different media influence reading processes. Third, hypertext appears to direct reader attention differently, perhaps focusing it on local rather than global structures. In this regard, it
might be equated more with poetic than with fictional forms. In any case,
as a hybrid, it invites certain forms of reading that are to be valued, and
teachers might view this as an opportunity to focus on style rather than on
structure.

Before I close, I should make a final observation. This chapter has
focused on hypertext reading; however, to return to the notion mentioned
earlier respecting the constructive, 'wreaderly' character of this medium, it
is worth remarking on the importance of encouraging students to engage
this medium both as readers and as writers. In my own experience with
students working with new electronic forms of literature, resistance to
literary hypertext dissipates when students are challenged to create their
own multi-directional creative works. Indeed, in my current work with
students reading hypertexts and writing (collaboratively and individually),
in malleable 'wiki' writing spaces, I often find those who are exceedingly
critical of hypertext structures as readers become wholly engaged as
writers, often delighting in engaging the rhetorical ploys they previously
eschewed. (I do not have the space here to take up a discussion of the
nature of wiki writing spaces; suffice it to say that wikis are open, some
might say anarchist, writing spaces that allow readers to edit web pages
easily in the browser. In my estimation they are one of the most promising
web-based writing spaces to emerge.) This disparity between what students are willing to accept as readers and what they are willing to produce
as writers, offers an interesting point of departure for discussions of how
reading and writing processes are both dissimilar and complementary.

References

Aarseth, E. (1997) *Cybertext: Perspectives on Ergodic Literature*. London: Johns Hopkins
    University Press.
Bakhtin, M. (1984) *Problems of Dostoevsky's Poetics*, trans. C. Emerson. Minneapolis,
    MN: University of Minnesota Press.
Barthes, R. (1974) *S/Z*, trans. R. Miller. New York: Hill and Wang.
Bernstein, M. (1997) Chasing our tales. Available at http://www.eastgate.com/tails/
    Welcome.html (accessed July 2001).
Bolter, J.D. (2001) *Writing Space: The Computer, Hypertext, and the History of Writing*.
    Hillsdale, NJ: Lawrence Erlbaum, Associates.
Brooks, P. (1984). *Reading for the Plot: Design and Intention in Narrative*. New York,
    NY: A.A. Knopf.
Chandler, D. (2002) *Semiotics: The Basics*. London: Routledge.
Derrida, J. (1976) *Of Grammatology*. Baltimore, MD: Johns Hopkins University Press.
Douglas, J.Y. (2000) *The End of Books – Or Books Without End?* Ann Arbor, MI:
    University of Michigan Press.

Eagleton, T. (1983) *Literary Theory: An Introduction*. Minneapolis, MN: University of Minnesota Press.

Iser, W. (1978) *The Act of Reading: A Theory of Aesthetic Response*. Baltimore, MD: Johns Hopkins University Press.

Jackson, S. (1995) *Patchwork Girl: A Modern Monster* (computer software). Watertown, MA: Eastgate Systems.

Jackson, S. (1997) *My Body: A Wunderkammer*. Available at http://www.altx.com/thebody/.

Johnson-Eilola, J. (1993) Control and the cyborg: writing and being written in hypertext, *Journal of Advanced Composition*, 13: 381–400.

Joyce, M. (1988) Siren shapes: exploratory and constructive hypertexts, *Academic Computing*, 3(4): 10–14, 37–42.

Kristeva, J. (1986) Word, dialogue and novel, in T. Moi (ed.) *The Kristeva Reader* (pp. 34–61). New York, NY: Columbia University Press.

Landow, G.P. (ed.). (1994) *Hyper/Text/Theory*. Baltimore, MD: Johns Hopkins University Press.

Landow, G.P. (1997) *Hypertext 2.0: The Convergence of Contemporary Critical Theory and Technology*, rev. edn. Baltimore, MD: Johns Hopkins University Press.

Lanham, R. (1993) *The Electronic Word: Democracy, Technology, and the Arts*. Chicago, ILL: University of Chicago Press.

Miall, D.S. (1999) Trivializing or liberating? The limitations of hypertext theorizing, *Mosaic*, 32(2): 157–71. Available at http://www.umanitoba.ca/publications/mosaic/backlist/1999/june/miall.pdf.

Miall, D.S. and Kuiken, D. (1994) Beyond text theory: understanding literary response, *Discourse Processes*, 17: 337–52.

Moulthrop, S. (1991) Beyond the electronic book: a critique of hypertext rhetoric, in *Proceedings of ACM Hypertext '91, San Antonio, TX, December 1991* (pp. 291–8).

Nelson, T.H. (1965) Complex information processing: a file structure for the complex, the changing and the indeterminate, *Proceedings of the ACM 20th National Conference* (pp. 84–100). New York, NY: ACM Press.

O'Faolain, S. (1980) The Trout, in *Collected Stories*, vol. I. London: Constable.

Rosenblatt, L. (1968) *Literature as Exploration*. New York, NY: Noble and Noble (first published 1938).

Snyder, I. (1996) *Hypertext: The Electronic Labyrinth*. New York, NY: New York University Press.

7

NEW TECHNOLOGIES IN THE WORK OF THE SECONDARY ENGLISH CLASSROOM

Colin Lankshear and Michele Knobel

Introduction

It is often observed that English classrooms continue to emphasize conventional writing forms at the expense of using new media to explore and realize the potential of multimodal text production as a means of communication, and for conveying information in factual (for example, exposition essays) and imaginative (for example, narrative) contexts. At the same time it is recognized that incorporating new media into curricular work should not be done simply for its own sake, but must be justifiable in terms of enhancing learning. This chapter identifies some considerations to be taken into account when deciding how, when and where to 'technologize' learning in English, and provides examples of the kinds of work that might be undertaken to good effect in terms of promoting worthwhile learning outcomes.

The (work of the) 'English classroom'

In recent years we have been interested to hear educators referring to 'the English classroom' in contexts where it had previously been more common simply to speak about subject *English*. While this might be more an idio-syncratic local perception on our part than a wider phenomenon of any significance, it nonetheless reminds us of the extent to which 'English' has become contested and diffuse terrain in curricular and pedagogical terms. Certainly, we think that the question of how, to what extent and why new media technologies, should be integrated into the *work of English classrooms*, is easier to get to grips with than the question about how, to what extent, and why they should be integrated into *English*. Indeed, in the context of writing about subject English as cultural studies, Dennis Sumara (2004) argues that the subject label 'English' is no longer sufficient as a descriptor.

Sumara's article reports discussions that took place, and conclusions that emerged, during a series of meetings of an English Studies Strand working group convened during the International Federation for the Teaching of English Conference in Melbourne, in 2003. The paper advances a number of ideas about the work of English classrooms that resonate closely with our own thinking about the role and place of new technologies within the work of learning. For example, the working group thinks of the English classroom as in part being a site for *producing* new forms of language and culture, such that the role of the English teacher will include 'helping students to *develop* interpretive tools and practices that exceed those used to examine printed texts, and are extended to other forms of cultural *production*' (Sumara 2004: 46; emphases ours). He also recognizes the centrality of identity work within English classrooms. From a cultural studies standpoint, 'English teaching emphasizes the relation-ship between literacy/literary practices and the ongoing production of human individual and collective identities' (Sumara: 46). Furthermore, the work of English classrooms must pay greater attention to 'technologies of practices' that are involved in organizing the production of know-ledge, since the artifacts used in teaching and learning have a strong influ-ence on how students 'develop knowledge about themselves and their contexts' (Sumara). According to this working group, the overall impact of approaching English teaching and learning, from a cultural studies per-spective, is to move towards 'acknowledging the complex ways in which the work in an English classroom represents not merely a representing or reproducing of culture but also, in profound ways, creates opportunities for the production of culture' (Sumara: 43).

The position we take in this chapter is that the secondary English classroom has become a home for a complex range of pursuits. Some classrooms engage in a wider range of purposes than others; some stay closer to traditional conceptions of English (literature, grammar), whereas others give greater emphasis to more characteristically 'contemporary' concerns. In short, most of the purposes addressed in the work of second-ary English classrooms would be covered by the items in a set, such as the following:

- Communicational competence.
- Literary appreciation (for example as literature scholars, as reader response).
- Aesthetic language use.
- Cultural induction.
- Linguistic mastery (L1 or L2).
- Function or genre mastery.
- Informational competence.
- Multimodal language competence.
- Identity work.
- Media savviness (consumers and producers).

This listing is not exhaustive, but it does point to some of the complexities associated with any discussion of 'English' classrooms and new technologies.

New technologies in the English classroom: critical perspectives

The secondary English classroom was not typically among the earliest starters in the take-up of computing technologies by schools in the early 1980s. It nonetheless became a conspicuous adoption site during the 1990s. This partly reflected the growing presence of media and popular culture studies within syllabus and curriculum statements for subject English from the 1980s. At the same time, it is probably fair to say that nowhere is the overall character of classroom appropriations of new technologies more apparent than in secondary school English. Three characteristics in particular define much of the current 'technology-mediated' work of English classrooms. We describe these in terms of 'digital busy work' (Bigum 2003b), 'digital pretend work' and 'digital conserving work', respectively.

'Digital busy work'

Chris Bigum (2003a,b) presents a general critique of school appropriations of computing and communications technologies since the 1980s. Bigum (2003a: 1) suggests that the history of computing within schools during the past 20 years has, mainly involved schools adopting 'a mechanistic approach, basically focusing on each new technology as it appears and attempting to find educationally useful things to do with it'. From this perspective, the role and challenge so far as integrating new technologies into pedagogical practice, is concerned essentially involves 'mastering the intricacies of each new technology as it appears' (Bigum 2003b: 2). This sets in motion, a never ending work agenda of identifying 'educational problems . . . for each new high tech solution' (Bigum 2003b: 3).

This approach has generated massive amounts of what Bigum calls 'digital busy work'. In digital busy work, learners use new technologies to perform *lower-order tasks* – such as locating information within sources provided by the teacher, in order to answer pre-set questions, or to render text generated by pen and pencil as web pages, or as ornate 'slides' created with presentation software. Digital busy work contrasts with the kind of work where learners integrate the use of the technologies into *higher-order challenges*, such as conceptualizing an issue or problem, designing strategies for addressing it, and evaluating the outcomes of implementing those strategies.

A large corpus of research evidence affirms that simply adding computers and the Internet to the routine classroom mix, does not by itself enhance learning (Cuban 2001). Nevertheless, the Internet is awash with recommended lesson plans promoting digital busy work in secondary English classrooms. Common generic examples of digital busy work include students presenting traditional book reviews as HyperCard stacks or PowerPoint presentations, where each slide is filled with text that the student reads to their classmates directly from the screen; constructing 'webfolios', series of web pages recording, for example, students' first year at high school (with sections dedicated to, for example: Favorite Assignments, My Role Model, My First Year in High School, Log of Books and Stories Read this Year); spending lessons online reading through seemingly random websites, whose URLs are posted online by their teacher as background reading to a new novel the class is about to start reading; teacher-generated websites to which students post narratives written as class assignments and so on.

Some concrete examples may help to clarify some of the issues at stake here. A popular commercial web archive of teaching ideas contains in its teaching guide and resource kit for Grades 6 to 8, an activity in which students present a PowerPoint presentation on an author's life (www. kidzonline.org/LessonPlans/lesson.asp?mode=0&UnitQry1=PowerPoint). Little guidance is given as to what makes for an effective oral presentation. Indeed, perhaps the most likely message to be taken from the student worksheet, accompanying the teaching guide, is that more is better. The guide encourages students to 'include facts, quotes, examples, images, sound clips, videos, and animations, that you think are important aspects of the topic'. It is unclear from the description of the assignment what distinguishes it conceptually from conventional paper-based biographical essays and accompanying posters about an author chosen (usually from a list of acceptable options) for study in class. It is unclear how inserting downloaded non-copyrighted sound clips, video clips and images, will add significantly to the assignment. The guide for students actually pays much greater attention to technical dimensions of using the software and Internet (for example, right mouse click to copy/paste – which, incidentally, assumes students are using PCs) than to explaining why author biographies can often help readers interpret their novels with more insight and sophistication. Furthermore, the online support resources engage students in completing templates for producing biographies (see, for example, www.bham.wednet.edu/bio/biomaker.htm) and searching online biography archives (for example, www.biography.com and amillionlives.com). The learning task effectively becomes an exercise in 'filling in the blanks' and seems to require little conceptual work on the students' part.

Bigum identifies webquests as a form of activity that has become popular in English classrooms, especially in the USA, and that often reduces to digital busy work (although at their best they can offer more than this). Webquests involve an approach to using the Internet in which teachers generate a task or problem that students can tackle using information from Internet sites, along with a range of offline resources, although this seems to be becoming increasingly rare. In the typical instance, says Bigum (2003b: 2), the teacher selects a set of online resources that students must use for solving the problem or completing the task. Bigum claims that this kind of digital busy work 'has characterized two decades of classroom computer use'. He argues that this can be construed by educators as a valuable form of educational engagement because 'students are using computers [and] because of the status of the technology outside of schools [this] must, in and of itself, be a good thing for students to do' (Bigum 2003b: 2).

Digital pretend work

To the extent that teachers themselves select the internet resources to be used in webquests, thereby precluding serious searching on the part of students, it is quite appropriate to regard webquests as a species of digital busy work. On the other hand, teacher-authors of webquests do not always circumscribe the online resources to be used, and it is not a necessary feature of webquests that they do. A webquest is simply 'an inquiry-orientated activity in which most or all of the information used by learners is drawn from the [Internet]' (webquest.sdsu.edu/overview.htm).

Traditional webquests comprise a set of teacher-generated web pages with six distinct elements or components: Introduction, Task, Process, Evaluation, Conclusion and Teacher Page. The Introduction sets the scene for the ensuing webquest. It typically takes the form of a 'scenario' or role for the webquester (for example, 'You are a detective in 19th-century London . . .') and usually ends with a question or problem that 'guides' the webquest. The Task provides a concise statement of expected end products (for example, a set of persuasive arguments for a hypothetical town council debate, a poster outlining a particular position on an issue, a newspaper editorial, archival selections and accompanying rationales for selection for a hypothetical historical society). The Process comprises guidelines for how the main task associated with the webquest is to be completed. It offers advice on where to start, and provides hyperlinks to online resources, tips on how to organize the information gathered and so on. Each step within the Process section is generally supported by a series of hyperlinks to relevant online information that will help students complete the task set for the webquest. The Evaluation provides information for students about how the learning outcomes for the webquest will be assessed, including assessment rubrics, teacher-generated criteria, student self-evaluation criteria, a 'points scale' and so on. Students are expected to use the assessment criteria to guide the completion of their final work product. The Conclusion can include a summary of what students have been expected to learn as a result of completing the webquest. It may also include additional prompt questions to encourage students to think beyond the webquest and extrapolate what they have learnt about other contexts and/or issues. The Teacher Page provides background information or 'metadata' on the actual development of the webquest itself for other teachers wanting to make use of this same webquest in their own classrooms. It typically contains information about which student groups it targets, which state or regional learning standards it meets, teaching notes, lists of supplementary resources and websites and even samples of students' work.

Within secondary English education, many webquests are devoted to exploring literary 'classics' or the contexts within which significant literary works were set or written. Trawling BestWebQuests.com yields 18 archived webquests for high school English classes (Grades 9 and 10 in this case). Of these, 15 make direct links to a 'classic' novel or text (for example, *To Kill a Mockingbird, The Crucible*) and ask students either to research historical background details or to transpose the book into a different genre (say, a screenplay) or a different context. For example:

> Imagine that you are a playwright and have just been approached by a wealthy man who wishes to sponsor a group of playwrights to rewrite a classic tale in a more modern setting. The tale must include love, revenge and betrayal. You batted around a number of ideas, but none of them fit the bill. Some had already been done before, others wouldn't translate well, but then someone mentioned Emily Bronte's 'Wuthering Heights'. A hush comes over the group as you consider this idea. The more you think about it the more you like the idea. It has all of those elements and character that will be interesting in any period!
> (bestwebquests.com/bwq/wqdetail.asp?wqcatid=3&edid=4&siteid=23)

This example reveals a second feature of much classroom work in general, and a lot of Internet-based activity within classrooms in particular: namely, its 'pretend' nature. So much of what learners are asked to do in classroom-based learning is simply not 'real'. It is almost as if recognizing that the classroom is a contrived, artificial learning context whose four walls drive a wedge between learning and life, words and the world, has become an invitation to *exaggerate* that limitation rather than to try to mitigate it. Learning takes on a kind of Disneyesque Fantasyland character, wherein students are asked to imagine themselves into all kinds of contexts they have no ken of, and to construct 'realities' or 'interpretations' using whatever information they can lay their hands on.

What is missing in such activities – what cannot be brought to any authentic kind of use of available artefacts and information resources – is access to the experiences and expertise (knowledge structures, formal procedures) that 'mature' practitioners of the activities in question (being a playwright, a movie director, a journalist, an historian) draw upon in doing their (*real*) work. Learners face the risk of a double mystification here. On one hand they are likely to come away from the activity with odd notions of what it is like to *be* in the manner of a playwright. On the other, they are equally likely to come away with odd ideas about how new technologies are employed in the worlds of playwrights, journalists and the like.

Digital conserving work

As Steven Hodas (1993) observes, schools are *organizations*. As such, they are interested in preserving and defending the way they operate. Their personnel will respond to stress in the system by trying to relieve this stress. The massive imposition on schools constituted by pressure to incorporate computing and communications technologies (CCTs) into classroom teaching and learning has been met by a 'persistent, teacher-centred notion about how CCTs [are to] fit into classrooms': namely, in ways that are 'in keeping with time-honoured classroom practises' (Bigum 2003a: 1). While not all teachers have responded to new technologies in conserving ways, there is nonetheless a powerful tendency in that direction – bolstered by the fact that many teachers still do not have a lot of 'insider' knowledge and experience of cultures of computing use. As a result, learning how to drive the new hardware and software applications as they arrive, and doing so within the context of familiar patterns and routines, has largely been the norm to date in classroom appropriations of computing and communications technologies.

A typical example of digital conserving work from a first-year secondary English classroom involves the recuperation of the venerable school newspaper project for activity in the computer lab. In one illustrative case, students are organized in groups of four or five in the computer lab and given the task of producing a four-page newspaper based on stories to do with the school. Within the 'teams', some members work on news stories, while others 'type' completed stories using desktop publishing software that aligns text in columns and insert clip art illustrations from a generic graphics menu that can be used to illustrate the articles. Individuals take turns at the different tasks over the production period. Predictably, students handwrite drafts into their English notebooks first before keying them on the computer, editing as they go and running the spell check before printing out their final draft.

Some principles to guide learning work in the secondary English classroom

In our attempts to find a basis for conceptualizing sound approaches to integrating new technologies into the work of English classrooms, we have developed several principles we think provide some useful guidelines. Four principles seem especially pertinent here. These are what we call the 'no hostaging' principle, the principle of 'efficacious learning', the principle of 'integrated learning', and the principle of 'productive appropriation and extension in learning'. We take these briefly in turn.

The 'no hostaging' principle

Curriculum and pedagogy must not be hostaged to technological change at the level of artefacts. To a large extent this has been the history of appropriating new technologies in schools to date. As we have seen, it has resulted in all sorts of contrived practises in order to find ways of accommodating new technologies to classroom 'ways'. This approach has not worked. It has 'wasted' the potential of new technologies to provide bridges to new forms of social and cultural practice that school education could and should be interested in, such as the so-called new literacies, multimodal literacies and so on. It has simultaneously 'wasted' the potential that new technologies have for doing, more efficiently, the kinds of familiar 'knowledge things' that schools *should* be engaging learners in, such as forms of analysis and synthesis associated with evaluating and producing knowledge in expert-like ways. The notorious 'web page and PowerPoint phenomenon' has dumbed the technologies down, maintained an out-of-date educational status quo, and turned off legions of students who refuse to have their digital sensibilities insulted in such ways.

The principle of efficacious learning

According to this principle, for learning to be efficacious it is necessary that what somebody learns *now* is connected in meaningful and motivating ways to mature or insider versions of *Discourses*. Discourses are understood as sets of related social practises composed of particular ways of using language, acting and interacting, believing, valuing, gesturing, using tools and other artefacts within certain (appropriate) contexts, such that one enacts or recognizes a particular social identity or way of doing and being in the world (Gee *et al.* 1996: 4). This involves thinking of education and learning not in terms of schools and children (place related and age specific) but, instead, in terms of human lives as *trajectories* through diverse social practises and institutions (Gee *et al.* 1996). To learn something is to progress toward a fuller understanding and fluency with doing and being in ways that are recognized as proficient relative to socially constructed and maintained (*proper*) ways of 'being in the world'. Participating in Discourses is something we get more or less right, or more or less wrong. Mature or insider forms of Discourses are, so to speak, 'the real thing': the way a Discourse is 'done' by 'mature users' who 'get it right'. They are 'authentic' rather than 'pretend' versions of the social practises in question. In this sense, for learning to be efficacious it must involve doing something that genuinely puts the learner on the right track towards becoming a competent participant in 'the real thing' – whatever the Discourse in question might be.

The principle of integrated learning

From a socio-cultural perspective, learning is integrated to the extent that three conditions are met. These all relate to the key idea that learning is inseparable from Discourses.

The first condition is that integrated learning occurs *inside* a practice rather than at a distance (as where one learns something *about* a practice as remove from participation in the practice itself, with a view to applying the learning *in situ* at some subsequent time). This is not to say that worthwhile learning cannot be decontextualized and subsequently applied, only that to this extent the learning is not integrated in the sense intended here.

The second condition extends the first. Learning is integrated when the various 'bits' of social practises that go together to make up a practise as a whole – and where the various 'bits' of related social practises that go together to make up a Discourse as a whole – are learnt in their *relationships* to one another, as a consequence of learning them *inside* the practise(s). In integrated learning we learn to put the various 'bits' (the speaking bits, tool- and artefact-using bits, action/behaviour bits, valuing and believing and gesturing and dressing and so on, bits) 'whole' and 'live'. We learn them *organically* in their relationships to each other, not as 'chunks' to be articulated later.

The third condition is that our learning is *the more integrated* the *less* it clashes with who and what we are and do, in the other discursive dimensions of our lives. The less that the 'identity' we are called to be in *this* learning instance is in conflict with the identities we are called to be – and are at home with – in the rest of our lives, the more integrated the learning can be. The example of Grace, described by Steven Thorne of Penn State

University, is apposite here. Trying to get Grace to learn conversational/ friendship French by means of email could not be *integrated* in this sense. Grace was, in effect, being asked to 'mean against' some of her other social identities and values that were (more) important to her. Other things being equal, the less conflict that learners experience between their social identities, the more effectively and willingly they learn.

The principle of productive appropriation and extension in learning

The principle of productive appropriation and extension in learning is partly an extension of the integrated learning principle, and partly the time-honoured principle that learning should build on what learners already know and have experienced. With respect to the first aspect, this principle involves looking for ways to reduce or ameliorate conflict between social identities during learning. For example, if an educationally acceptable appropriation of Grace's cultural construction of age-peer/ friendship communication (for example, via instant messaging) could be made within the French course, this would help integrate and strengthen her learning by putting cultural, personal, technological and epistemological aspects in sync.

With respect to the second aspect, if learners already know how to perform discursive roles and tasks that can legitimately be carried over into new discursive spaces, this can be used to advantage to enable learning and proficiency in a new area. For example, knowing how to archive downloaded music onto an MP3 player, such as an iPod, for personal entertainment purposes, can readily be transferred to archiving interview data files that have been recorded digitally for research purposes, without compromising either practice. The kinds of clashes between cultures of use, evident in the example of Grace described earlier, are not likely to arise in this case. Of course, this aspect of the present principle – building learning on, and integrating into present learning, relevant knowledge and competence, the learner already has – is practically self-evident. It is certainly widely recognized by educators. At the same time, it is systematically ignored or subverted on a massive scale within classroom learning. In an interesting counter-case, however, Duke University in the USA provided all its new freshmen for the 2004/05 academic year with iPods as 'part of an initiative to encourage creative uses of technology in education and campus life' (www.dukenews.duke.edu/news/ipods_0704.html).

Two scenarios for interpreting and applying the principles in secondary English classrooms

In the remainder of this chapter we want to tackle the question of what kinds of things might productively be done in secondary English classrooms to integrate new technologies into learning in ways that apply the kinds of principles we have outlined and, in the process, generate learning that avoids digital busy work, digital pretend work and digital conserving work. We will do this by means of two broad 'scenarios' or types of contexts within which teachers might be working.

The first is what we call a 'knowledge-producing schools' (KPS) scenario, named after an actual initiative operating in Australia which involves collaboration between academics led by Chris Bigum and Leonie Rowan, with several schools whose principals have accepted the KPS ethos as an ideal to be pursued by their schools (see, for example, www.deakin.edu.au/education/lit/kps).

The second is what, following Sumara, we call a 'cultural studies approach to work in English classrooms' scenario. In this broad kind of setting, teachers and learners are engaged in work that integrates new technologies into learning in ways that are consistent with ideals and criteria integral to a cultural studies approach.

A knowledge-producing schools scenario

Elsewhere (Lankshear and Knobel 2003a: 105–8; Knobel and Lankshear 2004: 78–105) we have described the small-scale KPS initiative that has been under development for several years now in Australia. The KPS have begun to develop new and interesting relationships with groups in their local communities, by engaging in processes that generate products or performances that are valued by the constituencies for which they have been produced. An important part of negotiating the production of such knowledge is that the product or performance is something that students see as being valued by the consumer or audience of their work. The students know their work is taken seriously, and that it has to be good or else it will not be acceptable to those who have commissioned it. The level of engagement and the quality of work and student learning to date have been impressive. These are not teacher-centred projects with peripheral student involvement. Rather, they are projects – in the sense in which the task of developing and producing a commercial movie or a new motor car are often called 'projects' – that are sometimes presented to students as problems to solve or, as has frequently been the case, problems the students have raised themselves with a view to solving them. The following are typical examples.

- Groups of Year 6 students worked in collaboration with the local cattle sale yards to produce a documentary of the history of the sale yards for a Beef Expo in 2003. They video-interviewed representatives of different sectors in the cattle industry, recorded *in situ* footage of activities, provided voiceovers and bridges between sequences and so on, and edited the components to produce the documentary as a CD. The product CD is being used at an international beef festival and by the local council to promote the region.

- A group of students interviewed local 'characters' and filmed them at tourist sites in an old mining town with high unemployment, and that is trying to establish itself as a tourist location. The students shot the film, edited it and burnt the product to CD. The data will be available at various sites around the town on touchscreen computers so visitors can get a sense of what the town has to offer. (Bigum 2003a: 5–6.)

- A group of Year 7 students from Waraburra State School in Central Queensland, received external funding from a Queensland Heritage Trails Network project budget to record video segments of interviews with some local 'identities' in a community named Mount Morgan – which was 'once home to the largest single mountain of gold on earth' (www.queenslandholidays.com.au/qhtn/attract_19.htm). The students filmed their interviews with the local participants on-site and edited the video segments. The video clips were then integrated into an interactive information 'quilt' that was hosted by the Mount Morgan 'museum without walls', part of the Queensland Heritage Trails Network. As one component of the project, the Waraburra students also tutored students from the local school at Mount Morgan on video filming and editing. A video segment created by the Mount Morgan students also featured in the quilt. Some of the funding received was used to acquire new sound equipment (lapel microphones and so forth) needed for this project because the students were not satisfied with the sound quality of previous projects. By the time of this project the students had already reached a level of expertise where they were attracting their own funding and having some say in how it should be spent, in order to improve the quality of their future work. The museum's report to the Queensland Heritage Trails Network Steering Committee stated that 'the oral history quilt has been installed successfully and has proven to be a hit with the visitors. The quality of the work done by the children is on a par with the professionals and is probably in fact more interesting as the children are visible and actually are asking questions of the interviewees. This is not the case in the others and some of the [other] segments could be considered to be rather rambling with no obvious editing taking place.'

Migrant Oral Histories Project

In this imagined example for students in Years 10 to 12, the four teachers and learners are working with two academics from the local university who have expertise in life history and oral narrative. A municipal council has commissioned a project to develop an oral history of the two longest established migrant groups in the city. This involves conducting life history interviews with elderly residents from the groups in question, focusing on their experiences of settling in their adopted land.

The English teachers and students have been invited to participate in the project as part of a local initiative to establish collaborative links between the university and the school. In this project the parties have established clear lines of roles, resources and responsibilities. The academics are primarily responsible for taking the teachers and students through the process of producing credible life histories. This includes such things as how to prepare appropriate interview schedules, how to use prompts and probes to elicit further information on aspects of life history that arise in the course of the interviews, how to obtain informed consent, how to organize and analyse the interview material, pursue follow-up interviews on relevant points at some later date as appropriate, and how to write up the life histories. This involves a series of working sessions, some of which are conducted in the classroom and some at the university.

The school has agreed to provide students to assist with data collection, as well as to assume responsibility for storing the data and for the infrastructure required to collect the data. This includes space on the school server, as well as use of the school's digital audio, video and photo recording equipment. The students and their teachers are also responsible for scheduling the interviews and for maintaining up-to-date records of work that has been done.

In a typical 'snapshot', two students are preparing for an interview with a couple. They are not sure about the appropriateness of one of their questions. They send an email message to the life history specialist they are working with, who sends them back some advice and also arranges to meet later with all the student interviewers to suggest ways of sensing when ground is becoming tricky during the interview. Importantly, she suggests that the students might like to 'clear' their questions with participants prior to doing the interviews, since this would also help the interviewees to prepare themselves for the interview itself.

Before interviewing begins, the school-based team establishes a website for the project. This will be used for archiving the digital sound and image files, as well as electronic copy of notes the interviewers make during the interview. It will also be used to organize and store other electronic material gathered from whatever sources that will provide pertinent contextual information for the life history project overall. It is envisaged that the 'project' will ultimately be 'presented' via a diverse range of media, including a dedicated website, and official CD-ROMS/DVD, journal and newspaper articles, a photographic and poster display, and selected image and sound 'bites' that will feature in digital touchscreen, information kiosks established by the city's tourist information bureau.

The school team also sets up a simple dedicated weblog for the project, to be used to maintain a record of all work done in the project. Participants (including the academics) are expected to make short posts to the weblog whenever an interview has been completed, when new material has been uploaded to the website, meetings have been held and so on. In this way there will be a permanent sequential record of how the project unfolded, of what has been done, of gaps to be filled, and of the roles played by participants.

One student has accepted responsibility for generally overseeing both the archival website and the weblog (blog) for the project. The website is a password-protected database containing all digital archival material generated in the project. It can be accessed by all team members for the various research purposes from any location with Internet access. These purposes include uploading new data, keeping tabs on what has already been collected (or not), to prepare data for analysis and printing out data to be analysed and generally maintaining a record of progress to date. It is not only the main digital database for the project, but also a potential future source of secondary data for subsequent projects upon approval, subject to ethical consideration. The student in question maintains this website, in collaboration with her counterpart in the university and her English teacher.

While all team members are registered and can post to the weblog, the same student follows up on comments and organizes the structure of the weblog. She also edits spelling, maintains the URL lists and generally performs the kinds of tasks undertaken by webmasters. The weblog serves as an audit trail for the project and as a repository of the team's thinking over time. As the project unfolds, team members blog ideas about patterns they are starting to see in the data, post links to online resources relevant to an aspect of the study, and list brief summaries, citations and location details of relevant offline resources (books, newspaper articles, artefacts in people's homes and so forth). The weblog also accommodates ideas, information and suggestions (for example, things to follow up, other people to interview, locations of documents and artefacts) relevant to the study posted by members of the public at large.

A third important electronic component of the project involves maintenance of the school's 'project reputation' system and of the registry of community expertise that has been made available to project teams. One student has accepted primary responsibility for maintaining these two systems, for all projects the school is involved in. On the basis of researching a range of well-known formal rating systems (eBay, Amazon.com, Plastic.com), this student (in collaboration with some friends at the school and two university students) has developed a five-point rating scale and a component for brief feedback statements. At the completion of each project he emails the 'client', providing a brief explanation of the rating and feedback system, a reference number, and politely inviting them to log their evaluation on the automated form on the school's project website. The clients enter their project reference number into the form (feedback cannot be left without this number), select a rating from a drop-down menu and provide up to 50 words of descriptive feedback in the text window. The student then updates the project reputation web page, which is public.

These ratings provide the formal public record of the school's level of performance as assessed by clients, as well as evaluative data on individual projects that contribute to team members' assessment portfolios. This public record of reputation is an integral part of the process by which the community develops a new perception of the nature and role of contemporary school education. The school recognizes that, to function effectively as a KPS, it (and other KPS schools) needs to be 'at least partially remade in the minds of the local community', and that 'project by project it [is] possible to build up a repertoire of [publicly recognized] research skills and products in consultation with local needs and interests' (Bigum 2002: 139).

The registry of community expertise that has been made available to the school in its project work, is likewise public and serves multiple purposes. In part it is a record of resources that might be available to the school and/ or other (non-profit) community groups for appropriate future activities. It is also a mechanism for community networking. In addition, and very importantly, it provides a public statement of the community service/ collaborative-cooperative dispositions of those who have demonstrated their recognition that education is the responsibility of the whole of the community. The record of projects on the school website simultaneously identifies those community groups and organizations that have supported the reconstitution of education as 'mature' knowledge production by commissioning projects.

In another typical 'snapshot', a pair of students who have just interviewed a couple are ready to enter the data. One of the students connects the small digital recorder (with inbuilt camera) to a computer with the necessary software in the classroom (or at home, in the school computer lab, at an Internet café or library) and uploads the digital audio and image files. When the upload is complete she logs on and FTPs (that is, uses a rapid transfer software application to send) the file to the project website for archiving. Her partner meanwhile logs onto the Internet and posts a short message to the project weblog, notifying that the interview has been completed and the relevant files sent to the website.

Each student is responsible for interviewing one person (or for interviewing couples in pairs). Having completed and archived their interview they listen to it several times, transcribe it verbatim, and send it to the interviewee, inviting comments, clarifications and amendments. While listening to the recordings they are looking for 'themes' – recurring motifs, ideas, matters of distinctiveness, emphases and so on – that will provide an interpretive structure and point of view (or perspective) for subsequently representing the life history in the narrative 'write-up'. The narrative might aim for wider coverage – a 'big life picture' – or it might focus on something narrower, such as a profoundly formative experience, a relationship, a working life.

After listening to the recording several times and spending a lot of time with the transcripts, students can make preliminary decisions about the kinds of themes they think are most important. They think about and discuss with one another and their teacher(s) how the words of the interviewees support the interpretations made and might be used – for example, as succinct quotations – to help 'carry' the interpretive line. With transcripts in place and themes identified, the students arrange to discuss their ideas with the academic partners by sending out electronic copies and arranging meetings. During the subsequent process, which might extend over several weeks, students, teachers and academics negotiate themes and lines of interpretation (making 'sense' of the 'lives' entrusted to them). They also negotiate appropriate procedures for including the interviewees in 'checking' lines of interpretation.

Not all life histories necessarily lend themselves equally to the same forms of 'write-up' and 'presentation'. Particular life histories might lend themselves to extended written presentation in print text (in oral history journals, newspaper stories and so forth) and/or as files that can be read online. Others may lend themselves best to vivid video presentations assembled as short segments of 'footage' (for example, of artefacts, relevant scenes, images of people or events) with 'voiceovers' spliced from the original interviews. Others again may (also) lend themselves to still photographic and/or poster displays. Complementary or contrasting life histories might be combined as 'moments' in larger and more complex representations of group life in the community. In a series of meetings and working sessions (or, electronically, at distance – building up a network of 'critical friends'), the teachers and students discuss with academics, and other persons from the community with relevant expertise, aspects of design for Web presentation, video editing and presentation, photographic collage and so on, in the attempt to achieve the best balance between expert-like media presentation (whatever the media in a given case) and faithful rendition of the life histories. The interviewees themselves may also want to be involved in this stage, and appropriate arrangements must be made for negotiating their 'satisfaction' with the sense made of their life histories.

A 'cultural studies approach to work in English classrooms' scenario

The concept of a cultural studies approach to English teaching and learning, mentioned at the start of this chapter (Sumara 2004: 43–6), foregrounds the idea of learning in the English classroom being seen as 'not only the "representing" of culture but also the "producing" of culture'. A cultural studies approach views the English classroom as being partly, but very significantly, a site for producing new forms of language and culture, and for exploring the relationship between literacy/literary practices and the ongoing production of human individual and collective identities, such that what is *produced* in the English classroom includes new experiences of identities that co-emerge with what is studied. Sumara's account of this ideal further specifies that, from a cultural studies perspective, 'the teaching and learning of subject matters are understood as explicit ways of "changing the subject" – where "subject" is understood broadly, as both product and producer' (Sumara). Within this conception, a cultural studies approach to English teaching 'also views the products of teacher and student engagements with different forms of texts as profound creative means of cultural expression' (Sumara). At the same time, however, this is not a simple matter of any kind of product at all counting equally as an outcome or achievement. The working party emphasizes the need to develop programmes in English classrooms that enable students to develop 'an informed and disciplined relationship with poetic/dramatic/ prosaic forms, including those that are organized and shaped by new media and computer technologies' (Sumara).

Within this broad framework of ideals and values we think the following examples represent productive ways of integrating new media and computing technologies into the work of the English classroom. Myriad further examples, including some that articulate more obviously and directly to traditional concerns of subject English, such as engaging with the literary canon, and others involving contemporary popular cultural forms, such as electronic zines, could readily be produced. These, however, must await other opportunities for discussion.

Weblogging as reflective and informed identity work

A weblog – or blog, for short – can be defined as 'a website that is up-dated frequently, with new material posted at the top of the page' (Blood 2002a: 12). There are many different kinds of weblogs serving quite different purposes. In the previous section we advocated using a weblog for the very functional purpose of maintaining a record of tasks undertaken within a team-based project. This, however, is quite an idiosyncratic use of a weblog – not least because most weblogs are written for much wider public audiences.

Most contemporary weblogs are hybrids of journal/diary-style entries and annotated hyperlinks, or some other kind of mix of musings, reflections, anecdotes, recounts and so forth, with embedded hyperlinks to related websites. Rebecca Blood (2002b: x) describes this new use of weblogs as being concerned with creating 'social alliances', in the sense that weblogs are largely interest-driven and intended to attract readers who have (or would like to have) the same or similar interests and affinities. Weblogs of this type can be seen as important forms of identity work. We can explore the identities projected by other people by reading their weblogs and, equally, we can explore and express aspects of our own identities by and through weblogging. In addition, weblogs typically include a comments function, so that anyone reading a particular entry or post can comment on it and have that comment available to other readers of the same weblog.

As we have discussed elsewhere (Lankshear and Knobel 2003a,b; Knobel and Lankshear 2004), the weblog has become the 'latest new thing' to be identified as an application for which classroom uses can be found. As with other applications that have gone before it (web pages, presentation software and so on), most of the school-based weblogs we have located are, conspicuously, *schooled* weblogs. Many show familiar signs of lacking any clear and strong sense of purpose. Student posts often look more like something that has been done as a requirement than they do thoughtful attempts to say something one wants to make available to others (known and unknown) on the grounds that they may be able to relate to it in a significant way. (Interestingly, many school-based weblogs do not even enable the comments function.) One school-based posting read:

'helloooooooooooooooooooooooooooooooooooooooooooooooooooooooo ooooooooooooi just dropped in to say a gigantic enormous helloooooooooooo. Good bye to you and you and you.'

In another case a student posted the information that she is updating her weblog from New York (where she is visiting on a trip). That is all the post says. There is nothing about her trip, about New York – simply the statement that she is updating from New York.

Another example seems to confuse weblogging with instant messaging:

Where is everybody? Hi, everyone . . . have got my guitar lesson in 20 minutes. Crazyland isn't so crazy anymore and furthermore . . . the login button has gone!! So I cannot access it from anywhere except my home. Glad you got those grades Cliff J. Bye.

Elsewhere, a class weblog – in which it is apparent that only one person has the authority to make the posts, and other students send copy to be blogged – reports that:

Our math class is working on converting fractions to decimals then to percents, mixed number and improper fractions. We had an extra credit challenge of cooking something at home, bringing it to class and dividing it equally among our classmates.

It is difficult to see any educationally worthwhile purpose reflected in this kind of weblogging, and in no way would we want to encourage English teachers to integrate weblogging into classroom activity if it results in such 'work'. Moreover, while there are no hard and fast rules and criteria for weblogging as a social practice, 'insider' perspectives on the qualities of effective weblogs are readily found on the Internet, along with information about which weblogs are most highly regarded. Serious bloggers are committed to carefully crafted, well-informed posts. Advice to novice bloggers usually emphasizes the need for accessible and succinct writing, and for style and design to complement each other. 'Readers [of weblogs] come from a variety of backgrounds. Write to the point, be simple and short . . . Usually I spend a minute or two on a weblog to see if there is anything new and interesting. You probably have 30 to 45 seconds to get a user's attention' (Shanmugasundaram 2002: 143). Having a consistent style in terms of font type, text layout and the like 'helps in [drawing] readers' attention to a specific area', and having 'a unique style of writing helps in getting regular readers'. From the standpoint of 'insiders', the cardinal weblogging sin is to be boring. This is referred to as the 'cheese sandwich effect', where weblogs operate at the level of describing what their writers had for lunch that day.

Of direct relevance to our argument at this point is the fact that it is possible to locate very easily a wealth of outstanding weblogs that engage in sophisticated identity work. Just as there are powerful search engines for locating resources in general on the Internet by using keywords, so there are specialized searching tools for locating weblogs that may deal with topics of personal interest to the searcher. These include 'metablog' sites such as Technorati.com, as well as the search functions provided by weblog hosting sites (for example, www.livejournal.com/site/search.bml). In addition, Google (www.google.com), which owns Blogger.com, a major weblog hosting service, is also an excellent resource for locating weblogs according to interests. Searching mechanisms draw on weblog authors' descriptive profiles to source weblogs by keyword or by interest. In addition, metablogs also enable Internet users to identify the 'top' weblogs according to specific criteria – such as Technorati's Top 100 popular weblogs ranked by inbound hyperlinks, which is accessed under the Services menu on the Technorati page (www.technorati.com). Other similar indices can be found at Blogdex.com, Eatonweb.com, Bloglines.com and the like.

Given the abundance of exemplary weblogs that 'do' identity work, and of search mechanisms for locating such weblogs, it is possible for English classrooms to address identity work as *an educationally valuable and relevant pursuit* by using weblogs in two complementary ways. First, existing identity work weblogs can be located and researched in order to study how they do this identity work, how well they do it, and by what means they do it. Second, learners can create their own weblogs for the purposes of undertaking identity work by exploring and expressing their subjectivities: projecting aspects of who they are, how they see themselves, the subject positions they experience the world from and so on.

As good a place as any to start is with a weblog like *Little.Yellow.Different,* which won the overall Bloggies award for excellence in 2003 (see www. littleyellowdifferent.com). *Little.Yellow.Different* was begun in June 2000 and is authored by Ernie Hsiung, a 27-year-old, self-described short and overweight, gay, Chinese-American web designer and developer who works for Yahoo!. It is a regularly updated, journal-like space that Hsiung uses to keep readers in touch with renovations he is making to his recently purchased apartment, events in his life (such as purchasing his apartment, appearing on a television game show, a trip to Disney World, subscribing to cable television, starting his new job with Yahoo!), accounts of his relationships and interactions with his parents and relatives, and general comments on popular culture. While many journal-type weblogs (which tend to be heavy on accounts, drawn from the author's life and light on annotated hyperlinks) have been criticized as being banal celebrations of mediocrity and the microinformation of everyday life, *Little.Yellow.Different* has attracted a strong following keen to read Hsiung's semi-regular, often hilarious accounts of what has been happening to him lately.

The design for Hsiung's weblog is polished and elegant (see Figure 7.1). In its default mode, the main body of the weblog is white, set against a two-tone green background (which he refers to as a 'dull puke olive color'). The font used throughout the weblog is clean and easily read. The main title banner for the page shows an artful 'ghosted' image of Ernie, and holds

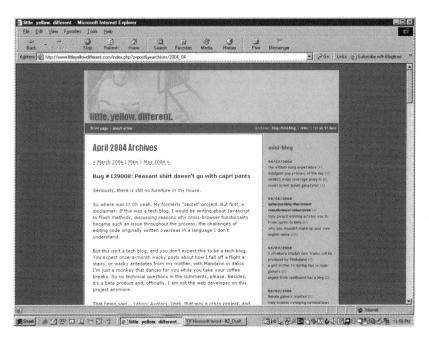

Figure 7.1 A screen shot of *Little.Yellow.Different* (www.littleyellowdifferent.com)

most of the navigational links for the weblog. These links access Hsiung's biographical data, archives of previous posts, and a section where readers can change the entire look of the weblog by swapping templates or 'skins'.

Many of Hsiung's posts are peppered with transcripts of real and imagined conversations or events, and each transcript is written in a dark grey font which sets it off clearly from the author's commentary. The comments for each post are accessed by clicking on a link at the end of each post, and are displayed in chronological order. Running down the side of the main weblog section is what Ernie refers to as a 'mini-blog'. This is where every few days he lists hyperlinks to websites he finds noteworthy.

Hsiung deliberately keeps his weblog non-technical, despite his own obvious interest in the technical side of Web programming and development. Reading this weblog over even a short period of days reveals important recurring themes in the posts. These include:

- Different challenges and benefits to be had from growing up Chinese-American.
- Contrasting his own experiences growing up Chinese-American with media representations of Chinese-Americans (including Chinese-American representations of Chinese-American culture).
- Gay cultural practices (including spoofing his own gay identity by way of confessing certain musical tastes, romantic attractions, interior decorating motifs and so on).
- Comments on popular culture trends and events.
- Finding humour in almost everything that happens to him.
- Keen-eyed observations on a range of social relationships, including those he has with work colleagues, friends, family and relatives.

Hsiung's accounts of navigating American and Chinese cultures are often deeply ironic (and infinitely patient) and regularly offer insights into what it means to be on the receiving end of mainstream America's tendency to homogenize all 'Asians'. His practice of recounting word-for-word dialogue in his posts becomes the perfect medium for both unveiling cultural ignorance, on the part of others, and for making pointed social commentary without resorting to blunt-edged, heavy-handed criticism. For example, he recounts an exchange at work as follows:

Engineering lead:	We don't have a lot of time to finish this project. It's a good thing another country has implemented an avatar system already.
Ernie:	(looks through code) Uhm, this is a lot of code. And these javascript comments are in Korean.
Engineer:	But aren't –
Ernie:	. . . I'm *Chinese*.
Engineer:	Oh. This project is still due next Tuesday.

Another post from *LittleYellowDifferent* (29 August 2004), presents Hsiung's often hilarious insights into life as a gay male working in an industry more known for its (stereotyped) intensely heterosexual and testosterone-charged male, and provides a quick tour of 'weblogging-as-identity-work' at its very best. Ernie was a key designer and programmer in developing the avatar figures for a new Yahoo! Online service. Once the beta, or trial, site was launched, Ernie was able to offer some interesting insights into what had, until then, been classified information concerning the backroom development of the website. He recalls how early versions of the male avatars he drew and developed caused some consternation among his male colleagues. He describes the scene as follows:

(The scene: Back in my cubicle. 7 guys are crowded around my computer, eagerly awaiting what the initial avatar drawings would look like.)

Ernie:	So, I choose 'male' for my avatar gender, press the 'Create my Avatar' button, and . . .
All:	. . .
Guy #1:	Oh my god, is he wearing daisy dukes?
Guy #2:	. . . and a wifebeater. The caesar haircut and the pouting aren't helping, either.
Guy #3:	Uhm . . . these avatars look pretty . . .
Ernie:	Homosexual?
All:	Yep.

(http://www.littleyellowdifferent.com/?z=post&y=
archives/2004_04)

The bottom line for trying to integrate new technologies into identity work within a cultural studies approach to English teaching and learning, via weblogging, is that it must be justifiable on the grounds of being educationally worthwhile. This means that the 'writing-as-exploration-and-expression-of-subjectivities/identity', must be undertaken *seriously*. This means, in the first instance, that our classroom webloggers must have the will and interest to take on weblogging as hard and challenging work. In other work (Lankshear and Knobel 2004) we analysed three highly successful weblogs to provide a preliminary account of what we think are integral features of effective weblogs. The first criterion, we identified for effective weblogs, is that their authors have a strong sense of purpose: a sustaining reason or motivation for producing and updating the weblog on a regular basis. Unless its creator has an authentic purpose – however whimsical this might be – a weblog is unlikely to survive the demands on time, energy, resourcefulness, affiliation and other forms of identity work, inherent in maintaining an enduring and effective production. This is the first aspect of *seriousness*. Learners must experience identity work as motivating and sustaining. This is not uncommon among adolescents and young adults.

Of course – and this is what makes weblogging so appropriate for identity work – students and teachers will engage more successfully in identity work to the extent that they have a sense of their own *point of view*. Identity and point of view, are indexical to each other. We regard having a recognizable and well-informed point of view as a second criterion for effective weblogging. Indeed, point of view is central to what weblogging is about: a weblog without point of view is practically a contradiction in terms (Dibbell 2002). Exemplary weblogs demonstrate the role and importance of a coherent and identifiable point of view against which readers can 'rub' and even 'test' their own values, beliefs, experiences, worldviews and so on. Point of view involves the projection of subjectivities. Hence, effective weblogging involves the capacity to articulate subjectivity, succinctly and in three dimensions, within the confines of one's chosen format for posts. To this extent, helping learners clarify and elaborate their points of view becomes a key element of effective pedagogy in the domain of identity work.

Finally, there has to be room for learner-blogger-identity-workers to 'grow': to get 'better' at doing identity work. This can be enabled, to some extent, by spending reflective time working with exemplary weblogs presented by other people. Ultimately, however, it requires one's own production. This, however, is production within a context where there is, simultaneously, exploratory experimental space *and* opportunity for sympathetic peer review and encouragement. This could almost be a partial definition of blogspace. The blogosphere is full of people looking for others to interact with. And many of these people are generous with their support and encouragement. At the same time, one is more likely to find those other people if one's weblog already shows some signs of promise. This is where the *quality of presentation* in a weblog – our third criterion for effective weblogs – can play an important part. Striving for an aesthetic that suits the 'feel' of the weblog one wants to create, and that shows care and respect for other bloggers as discerning people, becomes an integral part of the learning experience here. This, furthermore, is an educationally valuable objective. In minimal technical terms it entails thinking about templates, making decisions about the degree of customization one will pursue, and how to learn what is required for proficiency. In more 'maximal' terms of identity work in theory and in practice, it may entail the kind of thinking and competence inherent in Ernie Hsiung's device of allowing readers to swap 'skins' on his blog: to bring elements of *their* subjectivity to elements of *his*. It shows a deep awareness of what identity work is all about – bringing humour, point of view, and technical and aesthetic aspects of presentation together in a coherent statement of who (at least in part) one *is*. Anybody who fails to see how important his capacity is as a contemporary *credential* has failed to grasp the nature of our times.

Reviewing as cultural expression: towards 'expert-like' production of a textual form

In this concluding part we project into contemporary spaces one very traditional type of activity from the English classroom: writing reviews of books and other texts.

Reviewing is an everyday social practice that has always been associated with norms of expertise. Indeed, within formal published media the role of reviewer as a kind of public critic/intellectual who has typically been limited to those who are recognized as having the right credentials. Becoming a reviewer has traditionally been something to which a small minority of people might aspire – so much so that in, for example, academic careers, being asked to review published books, reports, films, exhibitions (and/or articles submitted for publication) constituted an important item on a CV to be taken seriously for purposes of getting a job or being promoted. The kinds of credentials needed for becoming a reviewer included literary capacity, recognized expertise in a field, respected point of view, mastery of reviewing as a genre and, in some cases, a valued personal style or an idiosyncrasy that appealed to a particular clientele.

To a large extent this particular 'world' of reviewing remains much the same as described here. On the other hand, whereas it was once *the* world of public and published reviewing, the Internet has now made it into just *one* world of reviewing – and almost certainly a *minority* world of reviewing in terms of the numbers of reviews read on a daily basis. Today, e-companies, such as Amazon.com, actively build reviewing into their attempt to redefine the role of an active consumer of diverse products ranging from books, music CDs and movie DVDs, to electronic games and gamesware, to computing hardware, all manner of software and even household products. Anybody can write a review and, moreover, on sites like Amazon.com, can build up an entire portfolio of reviews (as well as win prizes for reviews). It is even possible on this website to get feedback on one's reviews (for example, 'five from seven people found the following review useful').

Under contemporary conditions, the highly traditional and longstanding practice of 'reviewing' opens out into all kinds of possibilities within which new technologies can be used in ways that do not reduce to busy, pretend or conserving forms of 'work'. The last things that should occur here in the name of meaningful classroom activities should be using a computer to key in a handwritten review or, even worse, 'publishing' a drafted or keyed review as a web page or a PowerPoint presentation. Rather, learners could be locating resources that deal with reviewing texts as a social practice, and comparing varying accounts (including for different kinds of products) of what counts as an effective or appropriate review and review format and under what kinds of conditions.

In the classroom this could begin by simply keying 'how to write a review' into a Google search (this search identified 12.5 *million* potentially relevant resources). The first web page on Google's returned search list alone offered a fascinating array of resources, ranging from a playful 'meta' perspective on reviewing as a practice from the standpoints of reviewer and reviewed (www.sers.cs.york.ac.uk/~tw/1), to serious 'how to review' guidelines that would be useful for senior secondary school learners (leo.stcloudstate.edu/acadwrite/bookrevpre.html and library.usask.ca/ref/howto/breview_write1.html), to pages that actively solicit online reviewers for (Australian) books (www.yara-online.org/main_pages/write_review.htm), children's software (www.childrenssoftware.com/forum), music/movies/books for a city council's online library page (www.dudley.gov.uk/council/library/feedback/reviews.asp).

Getting a sense of different kinds of reviews across different media and for different kinds of artefacts and audiences, likewise provides excellent opportunities for intelligent Internet searching and sampling. Students can pool the product or artefact review websites they use when deciding to make a purchase, and develop concrete criteria for reviewing products in useful ways for particular audiences. Alternatively, students might begin their analysis of review types, audiences and so on, by visiting a review portal, for example Yahoo!'s book review portal (dir.yahoo.com/Arts/Humanities/Literature/Reviews), or by starting from an eclectic list of site types, such as the following:

- *Electronic game reviews*
  http://www.gamespot.com/
  http://www.metacritic.com/
  http://www.gamerankings.com/

- *Movie reviews*
  http://movies.go.com/
  http://www.rottentomatoes.com/
  http://movies.guide.real.com
  http://us.imdb.com/

- *Book review portals/indices*
  Yahoo!: http://dir.yahoo.com/Arts/Humanities/Literature/Reviews/

- *'Popular' public book review venues*
  Amazon.com: http://www.amazon.com
  Barnes and Noble: http://www.barnesandnoble.com/bookbrowser/Welcome.asp?
  Book Page: http://www.bookpage.com/
  Book Spot: http://www.bookspot.com/

- *'Highbrow' public media review venues*
  National Public Radio: http://www.npr.org/templates/topics/topic.php?topicId=32

New York Times: http://www.nytimes.com/pages/books/
American Librarians' Association: http://www.ala.org/ala/booklist/booklist. htm

- *Specialist book or text reviews*
Transgender: http://www.alchemist-light.com/
Gambling: http://www.jetcafe.org/~npc/reviews/gambling/
Children's literature: http://www.carolhurst.com/titles/allreviewed.html
Manga: http://www.mangamaniacs.org/
Anime: http://www.animeboredom.co.uk/anime
Mobile phone ringtone reviews: http://reviews.cnet.com/Ring_tones/4520–3504_7–5024580–1.html
Zines: http://www.invisible-city.com/zines/

- *Academic reviews*
Education Review: A Journal of Book Reviews: http://edrev.asu.edu/index.html

- *Book review services*
http://www.bookwire.com/bookwire/
http://www.fanstory.com/index1.jsp

- *Personal book review websites*
Danny Yee: http://dannyreviews.com/
ZimmerBlog: http://www.wfzimmerman.com/index.php?topic=WhatsNewforBookLover
Ring of Book Reviews: http://www.geocities.com/Paris/Rue/3086/revring.html

Besides identifying different styles and forms of reviewing, accessing such sites will also enable students quickly to locate and compare different reviews of the same artefact in different kinds of 'publications' or for different audiences, and to consider where they would (want to) position themselves as a reviewer. Enabling students to choose the artefact they focus on, to review or to read reviews about, helps them to tap into expertise they may have or be developing in their out-of-school lives, with respect to an artefact or cultural practice (such as manga graphic novels, video gaming, anime, science fiction movies, thrift shop shopping, garage saling). However, instead of merely 'making space' for students' out-of-school interests, writing reviews develops analytic and evaluative skills and processes that are useful beyond school subject area domains.

As with weblogging, there are two sides to spending time online (as well as with conventional print review formats – how does an online 'review bite' compare with/vary from a 'book note' or an 'in brief' review in a conventional print medium?) in reviewing space. One side involves 'learning about' reviewing. This is *researching* reviewing as social/textual practice;

getting to know the practice by spending time amid the artefacts of that practice – reviews themselves, ideas about reviewing, responses to reviews, opinions about a particular review and so on. The other side involves 'learning to do' reviewing. This is *producing* review artefacts as social/textual practice; and producing reviews as 'moves' within what is now a highly plural practice that occupies multiple kinds of spaces within which 'expertise' can be acquired and exercised by people at large, rather than according to the market economics of 'expert elites'. Far from ending up as some kind of 'pretend' activity, a learner might identify an electronic or print text venue in which to 'place' their review, such that it has an authentic and purposeful 'life' and, like weblogging, become part of a person's identity-building kit – as an individual identity, and/or as part of the collective identity of an affinity group (such as users of freeware, or a particular kind of gaming community) or of a much larger community of practice (for example, the community of reviewers on Amazon.com).

Last writes

Much more could be said about each of the examples addressed under our two scenarios. And many other examples could have been addressed (and more adequately) under each scenario. Moreover, there are many more scenarios that could be envisaged and addressed under the theme of new technologies in the work of the secondary English classroom. However, we think enough has been said to advance the kind of case we want to make for integrating new media and computing technologies into English teaching and learning. With or without new technologies, much that passes for curricular teaching and learning in classrooms, is work that has limited meaning, purpose and connection beyond 'doing school'. It is so much 'busy', 'pretend' and 'conserving' work. Student disengagement has become a cliché, so common and widespread it has become. New technologies merely up the ante for what we should have faced long ago. This chapter presents a somewhat timid attempt at redress. If it does no more than provoke more compelling responses, it will have done its work.

References

Bigum, C. (2002) Design sensibilities, schools, and the new computing and communication technologies, in I. Snyder (ed.) *Silicon Literacies*. London: Routledge Falmer.

Bigum, C. (2003a) Schools as producers of knowledge. Paper prepared for the Victorian Schools Innovation Commission. Available at www.deakin.edu.au/education/lit/kps/pubs/vsic_aug03.rtf (accessed 30 September 2004).

Bigum, C. (2003b) The knowledge producing school: moving away from the work of finding educational problems for which computers are solutions. *Computers in New Zealand Schools*. Available at www.deakin.edu.au/education/lit/kps/pubs/comp_in_nz.rtf (accessed 30 September 2004).

Blood, R. (2002a) Weblogs: a history and perspective, in J. Rodzvilla (ed.) *We've Got Blog: How Weblogs are Changing Culture* (pp. 7–16). Cambridge, MA: Perseus Publishing.

Blood, R. (2002b) Introduction, in *We've Got Blog: How Weblogs are Changing Culture* (pp. ix–xiii). Cambridge, MA: Perseus Publishing.

Cuban, L. (2001) *Oversold and Underused: Computers in the Classroom*. Cambridge, MA: Harvard University Press.

Dibbell, J. (2000) Portrait of the blogger as a young man, in J. Rodzvilla (ed.) *We've Got Blog: How Weblogs are Changing Culture* (pp. 69–77). Cambridge, MA: Perseus Publishing.

Gee, J., Hull, G. and Lankshear, C. (1996) *New Work Order*. Sydney: Allen & Unwin.

Hodas, S. (1993) Technology refusal and the organizational culture of schools, *Education Policy Analysis Archives*, 1(10). Available at http://epaa.asu.edu/epaa/v1n10.html.

Lankshear, C. and Knobel, M. (2003a) *New Literacies*. Maidenhead: Open University Press.

Lankshear, C. and Knobel, M. (2003b) Do-it-yourself broadcasting: writing weblogs in a knowledge society. Symposium paper presented to the American Educational Research Association Annual Conference, Chicago, 21 April.

Lankshear, C. and Knobel, M. (2004) Planning pedagogy for I-mode: from flogging to blogging via wi-fi, *English in Australia*, 139: 78–102.

Shanmugasundaram, K. (2002) Weblogging: lessons learned, in J. Rodzvilla (ed.) *We've Got Blog: How Weblogs are Changing Culture* (pp. 142–4). Cambridge, MA: Perseus Publishing.

Sumara, D. (2004) Literacy and textual studies: English as cultural studies, *English in Australia*, 12(1): 43–7.

8

RESEARCH ON TEACHING SECONDARY ENGLISH WITH ICT

Richard Andrews

Background

One of the key articles on the state of computer use in secondary school English lessons is by Tweddle (1997). She charts the way that English teachers, through the 1980s and 1990s, used computer applications creatively, adapting them to their own needs. Pioneers in the field, such as Bob Moy, had developed programs like *Developing Tray*: a program which gave the cloze exercise a magic, similar to that of a photograph developing in chemical fluid. Most teachers, however, saw the computer as a glorified typewriter, allowing a more manageable and structural approach to drafting and redrafting via word processing. It was not so much the computer that brought about such practice – drafting and editing had been part of English practice since the early 1980s (see Andrews and Noble 1981) – rather, word processing on the computer enabled the realization of an earlier curricular advance.

At the same time, English teachers were aware of the limitations – and potential future limitations – of computers in the classroom. As an antidote to the idealistic enthusiasm, expressed by futurists about the impact of computers in the classroom, English teachers were asking questions like:

- What is the role of the teacher and what types of interventions are necessary and appropriate with a computer?
- How can the computer be used to scaffold learning and not constrain it?
- When, if ever, is the computer neutral?
- Do pupils achieve more when they use computers, in what areas and why?
- How do we recognize quality in learning when computers are used?
- How can we analyse the group interaction, learning and products that computers enable?
- What are pupils learning that we do not recognize or understand?

These questions were highly relevant in 1997; they are still pertinent. Tweddle charts the various initiatives that swept through schools from the early 1980s to the mid-1990s. Typically, these were taken up by enthusiasts and not evaluated or disseminated well, thus leading to an uneven spread of good English teaching with ICT, despite the efforts of the National Council for Educational Technology (NCET), later to become the British Educational Communications and Technology Agency (Becta). Without a curriculum framework to share and encourage computer use in English, and without a firm research base on which to build policy and practice, such patchiness was inevitable. Nevertheless, Tweddle's recognition that 'collaborative writing, "virtual" group working, composing with graphics and words, researching online' were distinctively new activities in the English classroom (1997: 11) set a marker in the mid-1990s for how far English teaching practice had developed since the early 1980s. She ends with a caveat that has turned out to be prescient:

> While it seems improbable that the next version of the National Curriculum for English will ignore such developments, there is no likelihood that their full implications will be reflected therein.
>
> (Tweddle 1997: 11)

As far as the curriculum in England is concerned, that indeed is the case. The National Curriculum (DfEE and QCA 1999) created a version of English for the first years of the twenty-first century, that is distinctly mid-twentieth century in conception. Although there is a generic requirement across the curriculum that pupils should be given opportunities 'to develop and apply their ICT capability through the use of ICT tools to support their learning' and to 'find out things from a variety of sources, selecting and synthesizing the information to meet their needs and developing an ability to question its accuracy, bias and plausibility' (as well as a number of other laudable aims), ICT is not seen as integral to literacy or to English as a subject. The potential of computers to stimulate group discussion – recognized since the 1980s as one of the benefits of the computers in the classroom, and ironically brought about by pupils having to share computers for collaborative work – is not mentioned in the 'Speaking and Listening' section for 11–16-year-olds. Under 'Reading', there is reference to print- and ICT-based information and reference texts, but not to literary work on computer or to digitization. And with regard to 'Writing' there is a marginal note in the National Curriculum (p. 38) headed 'ICT Opportunity', where 'Pupils could use a variety of ways to present their work, including using pictures and moving images as well as print'. ICT is still seen as marginal, peripheral; a tool that can enhance existing print literacy or, at best, be compared to it. It has the position that film and video still have: that of an additional medium that can be used to shed light on the central print-based literacy and literary curriculum.

I attempted a personal review of research on the use and impact of ICT in secondary English, in *Teaching and Learning English* (Andrews 2001: 122–44). Adding to Tweddle's list above, further practices which had emerged in the 1990s, through the interaction of computers and English, had been an exploration of hypertext and non-linearity in reading (and, to a lesser extent, writing and composing); facility with text processing, so that transformations from one genre or text-type to another (a well-established and possibly central activity in English lessons) became easier; multimedia composition, moving beyond the combination of graphics and words to hybrid forms, including the moving image, still images and sound; and the development of new research techniques for the Internet (for example via search engines, keywords).

It is perhaps the facility that computers offer the reader/viewer to *manipulate* texts that is one of the most engaging aspects of the new technologies at secondary level. In the 2001 chapter, I asked, and tried to answer, the question 'How does the computer screen facilitate the close connection between composition and critical literacy?'

> The simple answer is by allowing the reader/viewer to manipulate texts, change texts, interfere with the sacrosanct nature of texts; to change their shape, to change words within them, to split them up and reformulate them, to write into existing literary works, to join voices with another text, to create split column texts. Thus the 'dialogue' . . . between reader and writer, between text and writer/reader, is made an active and interactive one.
>
> (Andrews 2001: 137)

The chapter goes on to reflect on the implications of digitization for English as a subject, concluding that such a conception will move the emphasis away from the book and from fiction as the core of the English curriculum towards a more hybrid, less literary subject in which print literacy is seen as just one of a number of kinds of literacy. Even the rhetorical compositional sequence of substance followed by structure, then style, then presentation – reinforced by the drafting and editing approach to composition – is now under threat from a new approach to composition which starts with presentational issues, driven by considerations of audience: What is my audience? What format shall I compose in? What shape does that take? What shall I say? This seeming reversal of the usual route towards a piece of *writing* is interesting in that it moves closer to a conception of composition as *design*, as suggested by Kress (1997).

The above reviews of the impact of ICT on secondary English teaching and learning were largely personal and informal. In the middle section of this chapter, I draw on a more formal, explicit review of research on the impact of ICT on learning in English lessons.

The EPPI reviews

In 2001, a research team based at the University of York began work on mapping and reviewing research published internationally since 1990, on the impact of ICT on literacy learning in English for 5–16-year-olds. The systematic research review approach, using EPPI-Centre methodology, is detailed in separate reports: Andrews *et al.* (2002) on networked ICT; Burn and Leach (2004) on moving image literacies; Locke and Andrews (2004) on literature-based literacies, Low and Beverton (2004) on the impact of ICT on speakers of English as an additional language; and Torgerson and Zhu (2003) on the effectiveness of ICT in literacy learning, and in a book (Andrews 2004) that brought the five reports together with critical and methodological commentary. The reports and book focus on the 5–16 age range, and it is worth noting at the start of this section that the majority of research published during the 1990s and early 2000s has been on the impact of ICT in the primary/elementary years.

Of the 212 studies identified as relevant to the general interest in the impact of ICT on literacy learning (and thus to all the separate in-depth reviews noted above), 74 were undertaken in the secondary education sector. Sixty-three per cent of the 212 studies were conducted in the USA, 18 per cent in the UK, 8 per cent in Australia, 7 per cent in Canada, and the rest in New Zealand, Sweden and the Netherlands. Approximately two-thirds of the studies overall assume a psychological conception of literacy, namely one in which the process of becoming more literate is seen principally as an individualistic, internal matter. The remaining one-third see literacy as a sociological construct, thus developed through interaction with others. Given the predominance of social theories of language acquisition in the last quarter of the twentieth century, it is somewhat surprising to see the majority of studies using a psychological basis for their measurement of the impact of ICT on literacy learning.

Regarding the key terms in the review of research, 'literacy' was defined both in its narrow sense of the ability to read and write, and in two wider senses: first, in the sense that written language can include graphical and pictorial language as well as verbal language; second, in the sense of the ability to operate a range of cultural and/or social representations, thus leading to the use of the term 'literacies' to acknowledge the diversity of such literate practices. 'ICT' was limited to stand-alone computers with a multimodal interface, that is, networked and stand-alone computers, mobile phones with a capacity for a range of types of communication, and other technologies that allow multimodal and interactive communication. The term 'English' embraced English as a first or additional language learnt as a medium of instruction in school, at home or on the Internet – not as a 'foreign' language learnt, for example, in a modern foreign languages department. Finally, 'impact' was defined as impact on learners, rather than on institutions or curricula; and we decided to stay with the broadness implied by the term 'impact' rather than focus more sharply on 'effect' (except in the review by Torgerson and Zhu 2003).

The results of the systematic reviews are best read in the individual and full technical reports listed above, or in the book arising from the reviews. In the present chapter, I take a less systematic look at some of the papers that were based on English lessons in the secondary sector. My informal discussion is based on two of the five systematic reviews: one on networked ICT (Andrews *et al.* 2002) and the other on ICT and literature-based literacies (Locke and Andrews 2004). In this case, I will be looking at only those articles and papers reviewed that pertain to secondary or high school education.

First, it should be said again that the majority of papers on the impact of networked ICT on literacy learning and teaching in the period 1990 to 2002, focused on the primary or elementary sector rather than on secondary or high school English. This may have been because it is easier to research the 7–11 age group and their use of networked computers in school, than it is to research in secondary or high schools. Nevertheless, there are some papers – all case studies or series of case studies – that can be mentioned. Abbott's (2001) article on young male website owners, does not focus on classrooms as such but provides vignettes of three students who create their own websites at home. These three students act as 'types': the 'technological aesthete', the 'community builder' and the 'professional activist'. What the article shows, through detailed accounts of each of the students and their websites, is that identity is closely connected to the creation and maintenance of an online communicative presence. The implications for teachers of students like these is that knowing what literacy activities take place out of school, in electronic networked communities, is an important element towards understanding the capabilities and potentials of students in English.

Morgan's (2001) research, like Abbott's, is based on theories of situated practice and on social analyses of literacy. It looks at three teachers' classrooms and their practices. The essential findings are that because literacy is not a context-free skill, it is important for teachers to negotiate sociological factors that students encounter in their use of networked ICT in the English classroom; and that the opening of an ICT networked channel on textual work can add an extra dimension to the transformative possibilities that are so central to English as a subject. For example, a text in one format (such as a printed poem) can be transformed via an online dialogue into a more hybrid text that includes electronic annotation, visual analogies and illustration. Additionally, an implication of Morgan's findings is that a key sociological variable that influences networked ICT work in English is the presence of the teacher. In the classroom and school at least, teachers act as a mediating presence between the technology and the experience of language. Their values, disciplinary knowledge and pedagogical approach are critical to the student experience.

Similarly, the work by Bigum *et al.* (1997), which included research by Morgan, laid emphasis on specific situations in which networked ICT was deployed in Australia to enhance teaching in English. The report, *Digital Literacies*, assumes that the relationship between technology and literacy is symbiotic, with literacy practices affecting the design and use of ICT, as well as the other way round. Methodologically, case study – at least for the present – seems the best way to describe and analyse the emergent relationships that form between classes, ICT and English.

Echoing Morgan's work in a different way, the study by Love (1998) of a trainee teacher's work in a secondary English class in Melbourne, looks at how English teachers are using computers in their classrooms. There is particular emphasis in this study on the management techniques needed to maximize networked ICT use in English: one of the suggestions in the article is that English teachers need to think hard about when to, and when not to use (or encourage their students to use) networked technologies in (or outside) lessons. An example of such a judgement – my own example rather than Love's – is when a homework is set to research a topic, such as 'tragedy' or 'writing by John Agard'. Even with a fairly specific topic like the latter, there is a considerable amount of material on the Internet and it is useful to students and their parents to know what the scope of the search process is, and in what format (with what characteristics) the written work is expected to appear. Otherwise, students can get bogged down in information and be distracted from the key learning aspects of the assignment.

The last three papers mentioned above (Love 1998; Abbott 2001; Morgan 2001) were also included in the systematic review of the impact of ICT on literature-based literacies (Locke and Andrews 2004). Terry Locke and I wanted to see literature work in the English classroom as one of a possible number of 'literacies' that might be practised and studied, rather than as the heart of the English curriculum. We were aware, too, that an ICT dimension to literary study asked questions about the archetypal format for literature: the book. These would include questions, such as 'Does literature have to take printed book form, or can it be published electronically?' as well as more pragmatic questions like 'How might ICT enhance conventional book-based literature teaching and learning in the classroom?' One of the studies we looked at, was that by Meskill and Swan (1996) which trialled literature software packages in the classroom. The theoretical model underpinning the study was that of reader response; and the article explored 'the potential of a complementary relationship between the learning and teaching of literature, and characteristics specific to multimedia instructional delivery systems' (p. 218). Complementarity was seen to work both in the enhancement of the literary experience and in the effect on the design of literature software. Another relevant study, this time by a practising teacher, was that of Nettelbeck (2000), undertaken in a secondary independent co-educational school in Melbourne. This study revealed that there were a number of ways in which students could respond to literary texts, for example, in threaded discussions on texts, in online and offline written dialogue about texts, and in a process of accretive annotation of texts. Nettelbeck describes and analyses a classroom in which ICT is used in the service of literary understanding, and in which a community of learners is engaged in exploring literary texts in collaborative, informal and exciting ways. The readers/students approach the literary texts with a healthy irreverence, their 'voices' entering and commenting on the text and thus taking a place alongside it.

Implications for research, policy and practice

Research

There are plenty of implications for research, policy and practice as a result of what we know – and don't know – about the use of ICT in English secondary classrooms. One of the most useful aspects of systematic reviews is that they expose gaps in knowledge, or suggest where research might have been better carried out to answer a particular question. They are, thus, helpful in terms of ground-clearing and setting out new areas for research.

In research terms, then, there have been no large-scale empirical studies that have tried to determine the effectiveness of English with computers as opposed to English without computers. This finding is somewhat surprising in the light of claims made for the impact of computers on literacy learning and teaching. Generally speaking, there is an imbalance in studies in this field: we have a number of small-scale quantitative studies, and a number of small-scale, but not necessarily, in-depth qualitative studies. More breadth *and* more depth are necessary in research in the field. In addition to further empirical work, there needs to be a clearer, research-based look at the conceptual issues informing research into this topic. All too often the assumption is made (as it was when we did the five EPPI-Centre reviews on ICT and literacy in 2001–03) that ICT is the intervention and that it is impacting on literacy learning and teaching. In other words, the assumption is that there is a causal relationship, with the intervention (ICT) impacting on literacy which results in a change. However, it could be the case that the relationship between ICT and literacy is not causal but symbiotic; in other words, ICT and literacy impact on each other (as technology and literacy have been doing for centuries). Such an understanding requires a different kind of research approach, as I have suggested elsewhere (Andrews 2003a, b). Another important issue for research is that a distinction needs to be made between classroom-based studies and home-based studies. Much research in the field necessarily blurs the distinction between school and home because the use of computers, and particularly of the internet, opens up new electronic communities of learning that bridge home and school. But there are still questions that have to be answered about the best deployment of computers in schools, particularly as equity and access issues are less differentiated in school than they are at home.

Further issues for research include the question whether ICT is motivating only in the short term, or whether there are more medium- and long-term extrinsic motivational benefits to be gained. Other questions are about research itself into ICT and literacy: is it lagging too far behind technological development and classroom practice to be of any real use, other than in retrospective terms? Might research be better used to contribute to and inform future practice, for example, in research and development of new software or new websites, or even new hardware? Should research, as conventionally conceived, always be published in print, or should we look for hypermedia and multimedia formats for 'writing' about new developments in ICT and literacy? Finally, what about English as an additional language? What are the research implications for this important dimension of literacy in the early twenty-first century, whether English is learnt in England or in other countries? What contextual, social, economic and political issues come to bear on the question of 'English' and ICT?

Policy

Policy issues are specific to particular countries. In England, the main issue for the next policy rethink of the curriculum is whether ICT can be placed more centrally in relation to English and literacy learning, or whether it will remain on the edge of a basically nineteenth-century curricular creation that has literary study and print-based literacy at its core. A move to disconnect 'English' from its close connection with literary books would acknowledge the digitization of contemporary discourse, and the choices and transformations between text formats, genres and media that are so common now. If 'literacy' can be conceived as a capability in reading and writing (in the broadest senses, including the reading and composing of film, digital video and so forth), then questions of which medium, genre and format are used become secondary – but important – issues.

As suggested in the article by Tweddle (1997), policy makers get excited by short-term initiatives that are often poorly evaluated. One implication for policy, then, is to think medium- and longer-term rather than short-term, and to evaluate more rigorously. One form of evaluation that has, to date, not taken place internationally is a large-scale trial to compare the effects of ICT against non-ICT applications in the English secondary curriculum, or indeed to compare different ICTs against each other. A systematic review was initiated in 2003 to look at research published between 1998 and 2003, on the effectiveness of different ICTs on pedagogy in English teaching and learning for 5–16-year-olds (Andrews *et al.* 2004). Other recent reports on research literature on ICT, attainment and pedagogy, though not focusing exclusively on ICT and secondary English, are by Cox *et al.* (2004a, b).

Another aspect of policy that is often forgotten is that it may not be the technology that is at the centre of questions about classroom impact. Instead, the ideology, background and values of the teacher may be a more important factor. There are research implications here too; but in terms of policy, important issues of teacher preparation, competence and willingness to engage with new problems and challenges in the ICT classroom are central to the impact of ICT on literacy learning, and vice versa.

Practice

There is no substantial and solid evidence to show that non-ICT methods of instruction are inferior to the use of ICT, to promote literacy learning in English lessons at secondary level. The curriculum and its assessment are set up in such a way that – at least in England – pupils can succeed at the highest level in English as a school subject without recourse or access to a computer. At the same time, however, the National Curriculum, in England, requires that secondary pupils should use ICT to find things out, develop their ideas, exchange and share information, review, modify and evaluate their work. As suggested in the previous section on policy, it may be that the teacher is the key figure for pupils in terms of attitudes towards the use of ICT in English, at least in the curriculum and in the classroom. ICT certainly can change the role of the teacher from instructor to facilitator in some parts of the curriculum. Take the now time honoured use of word processing in the classroom and for homework. It is teachers who will determine whether pupils see the process of drafting and redrafting as a surface issue (accuracy, presentation) or as an opportunity to compose and recompose a piece of writing, or multimedia, in more depth. Behind such practices are ideas about the writing process, and these ideas are informed by the teacher's own perception about writing and composing (and perhaps by his/her own writing practices). The teacher, thus, continues to mediate between changing technologies and the act of writing or reading in the classroom.

Acknowledgements

I am grateful to Sue Beverton, Andrew Burn, Diana Elbourne, David Gough, Jenny Leach, Terry Locke, Graham Low, Rebecca Rees, Alison Robinson, Katy Sutcliffe, Carole Torgerson and Die Zhu, for joint work on the systematic reviews referred to in this chapter, and also for their permission in allowing me the space to reflect in a more personal mode on some of the issues regarding secondary school English.

References

Abbott, C. (2001) Some young, male website owners: the technological aesthete, the community builder and the professional activist, *Education, Communication and Information*, 1: 197–212.

Andrews, R. (2001) *Teaching and Learning English: A Review of Recent Research and its Applications*. London: Continuum.

Andrews, R. (2003a) ICT and literacies: a new kind of research is needed, *Literacy Learning: The Middle Years (The Journal of the Australian Literacy Educators' Association)* , 11(1): 9–12.

Andrews, R. (2003b) Where next for research on ICT and literacies? Keynote address, International Federation for the Teaching of English conference, University of Melbourne, July 2003.

Andrews, R. (ed.) (2004) *The Impact of ICT on Literacy Education*. London: RoutledgeFalmer.

Andrews, R. and Noble, J. (1981) *From Rough to Best*. London: Ward Lock Educational.

Andrews, R., Burn, A., Leach, J., Locke, T., Low, G. and Torgerson, C. (2002) *A Systematic Review of the Impact of Networked ICT on Literacy Learning in English, 5–16* (EPPI-Centre Review), Research Evidence in Education Library, 1. London: EPPI-Centre, Social Science Research Unit, University of London.

Andrews, R., Hou, D., McGuinn, N., Robinson, A. and Torgerson, C. (2004) The effectiveness of different ICTs in the teaching and learning of English, 5–16 (a protocol for a systematic review). London: EPPI-Centre, Social Science Research Unit, University of London.

Bigum, C., Durrant, C., Green, B., Honan, E., Lankshear, C., Morgan, W., Murray, J., Snyder, I. and Wild, M. (1997) *Digital Literacies: Literacies and Technologies in Education – Current Practices and Future Directions*. Canberra: Department of Employment, Education, Training and Youth Affairs.

Burn, A. and Leach, J. (2004) *A Systematic Review of the Impact of ICT on the Learning of Literacies Associated with Moving Image Texts in English, 5–16* (EPPI-Centre Review), Research Evidence in Education Library, 2. London: EPPI-Centre, Social Science Research Unit, University of London.

Cox, M., Abbott, C., Webb, M., Blakely, B., Beauchamp, T. and Rhodes, V. (2004a) *A Review of the Literature Relating to ICT and Attainment*. Coventry: British Educational Communications and Technology Agency.

Cox, M., Abbott, C., Webb, M., Blakely, B., Beauchamp, T. and Rhodes, V. (2004b) *A Review of the Literature Relating to ICT and Pedagogy*. Coventry: British Educational Communications and Technology Agency.

DfEE and QCA (1999) *English: The National Curriculum for England (Key Stages 1–4)*. London: Department for Education and Employment, and Qualifications and Curriculum Authority. Available at www.nc.uk.net.

Kress, G. (1997) *Before Writing: Rethinking the Paths to Literacy*. London: Routledge.

Locke, T. and Andrews, R. (2004) *A Systematic Review of the Impact of ICT on Literature-based Literacies in English, 5–16* (EPPI-Centre Review), Research Evidence in Education Library, 2. London: EPPI-Centre, Social Science Research Unit, University of London.

Love, K. (1998) Old cyborgs, young cyborgs (and those in between), *English in Australia*, 121: 63–75.

Low, G. and Beverton, S. (2004) *A Systematic Review of the Impact of ICT on Learners between 5 and 16, for whom English is a Second or Additional Language* (EPPI-Centre Review), Research Evidence in Education Library, 2. London: EPPI-Centre, Social Science Research Unit, University of London.

Meskill, C. and Swan, K. (1996) Roles for multimedia in the response-based literature classroom, *Journal of Educational Computing Research*, 15: 217–39.

Morgan, W. (2001) Computers for literacy: making the difference?, *Asia Pacific Journal of Teacher Education*, 29: 31–47.

Nettelbeck, D. (2000) Using information technology to enrich the learning of secondary English students, *Literacy Learning: The Middle Years*, 8: 40–9.

Torgerson, C. and Zhu, D. (2003) *A Systematic Review and Meta-Analysis of the Effectiveness of ICT on Literacy Learning in English, 5–16* (EPPI-Centre Review), Research Evidence in Education Library, 2. London: EPPI-Centre, Social Science Research Unit, University of London.

Tweddle, S. (1997) A retrospective: fifteen years of computers in English, *English in Education*, 31(2): 5–12.

INDEX